NO RECIPE?
NO PROBLEM!

NO RECIPE?
NO PROBLEM!

How to Pull Together Tasty Meals without a Recipe

PHYLLIS GOOD

Photographs by Keller + Keller Photography

Storey Publishing

The mission of Storey Publishing is to serve our customers by
publishing practical information that encourages
personal independence in harmony with the environment.

EDITED BY Deanna F. Cook and Sarah Guare
ART DIRECTION AND BOOK DESIGN BY Carolyn Eckert
TEXT PRODUCTION BY Jennifer Jepson Smith
INDEXED BY Christine R. Lindemer, Boston Road Communications

COVER AND INTERIOR PHOTOGRAPHY BY © Keller + Keller Photography
ADDITIONAL PHOTOGRAPHY BY Artur Kornakov/Unsplash, 217; Courtesy of the author,
    back cover (author); Carly Jayne/Unsplash, 171; © ehaurylik/iStock.com, 189; Fa Barboza/
    Unsplash, 191; foodism360/Unsplash, 49; © Lara Hata/iStock.com, 58; © Lilechka75/
    iStock.com, 188; © Olga Peschkova/iStock.com, 322; © pinstock/iStock.com, 43;
    © Tatiana Volgutova/iStock.com, 31
FOOD AND PROP STYLING BY Catrine Kelty
ILLUSTRATIONS BY © Jen B. Peters

TEXT © 2021 BY PHYLLIS GOOD

Storey books are available at special discounts
when purchased in bulk for premiums and
sales promotions as well as for fund-raising
or educational use. Special editions or book
excerpts can also be created to specification.
For details, please call 800-827-8673,
or send an email to sales@storey.com.

STOREY PUBLISHING
210 MASS MoCA Way
North Adams, MA 01247
storey.com

Printed in China through World Print
10 9 8 7 6 5 4 3 2 1

Library of Congress Cataloging-in-Publication
   Data on file

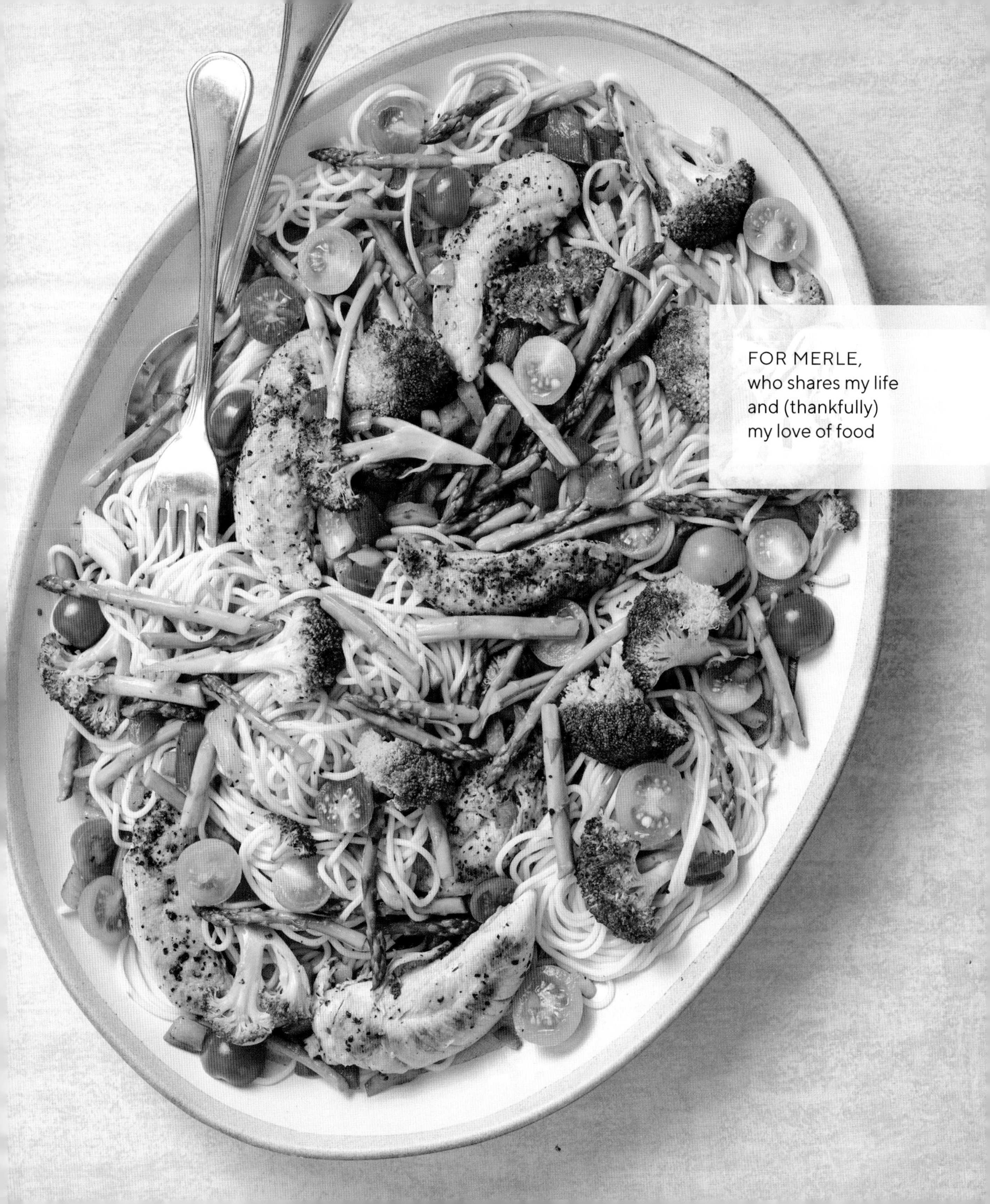

FOR MERLE,
who shares my life
and (thankfully)
my love of food

CONTENTS

INTRODUCTION TO FREESTYLE COOKING

WELCOME TO FREESTYLE COOKING, where ingredients lead the way and you get to improvise—just like a jazz musician. Where you get to experiment with whatever technique you choose. Where you serve up dishes that come together in surprising harmony.

Great jazz musicians start with a theme. They try it out. They add a few riffs. Something new floats up, and they weave it in. Or they let it call them in another direction. And so they go on, experimenting, trying things. It's a let's-see-what-happens approach—open, full of surprise, yet drawing on what the musician already knows.

With this style of cooking, you bring the theme—the ingredients. They help suggest what happens next. You think about what each ingredient has to offer. You take your time. You find your way.

How do you decide what to do next? When I think about what to cook for dinner, three questions usually show up:

1. What am I hungry for?

2. What do I have on hand?

3. How much time do I have?

With a quick check of my fridge, pantry, countertop, and freezer, I become pretty clear about the answers to the first two questions. Then I figure out what form and cooking method will work best with what I found and the time I have. A soup, a bowl, a pizza, a sheet-pan dinner? A salad? A toast topper? Now I'm ready to start cooking—freestyle jazz cooking!

About This Book

I offer three assists throughout this book, in case questions come up or you'd like a little company while you cook:

Freestyle cooking ideas appear in many of the chapters. Think of them as kick starts, or possible ways to begin and then go on to create a dish. I imagine the Freestyle cooking ideas as scaffolding—ways to get your bearings as you get going and then ultimately set a finished dish on the table.

Essential Techniques are where you'll find helpful, hard-core information—for example, the best ways to cook an egg, the best oven temperatures for roasting vegetables and big proteins, and the ratios of liquids to dry ingredients for cooking grains.

Following the Freestyle cooking ideas and Essential Techniques, you will find specific ideas to stoke your imagination. These are combinations of ingredients you might want to experiment with using together, ways to prepare food you may not have tried before, and ideas for respecting food by the way you handle and prepare it. Think of these as suggestions, with some hints for success. They simply offer you a place to begin!

The Cooking Circle is a group of 14 experienced improvisational cooks from across the country who became a virtual cooking community when I invited them to share some of their cooking ideas and stories with me for this book.

These people are a community of riches—each one cooking in his or her own way—who will give you encouragement all along the way, plus new ideas you haven't yet thought of. Their many tips, hints, and stories come from their vast and varied cooking experiences. You'll see Tips from the Cooking Circle and their names throughout these pages. The rest of the material? It comes from me!

BETH, from Pennsylvania, is a high school teacher.

CHRISTINA, from Pennsylvania, is a democracy advocate.

CHUCK, from Kansas, is an urban farmer and museum exhibit designer.

DARYL, from Pennsylvania, is a natural-disaster crisis manager.

EUGENE, from Florida, is a retired fashion designer.

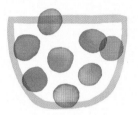

EVONNE, from Virginia, is a retired nurse and now a gardener, cook, and baker.

GINI, from Ontario, is a culinary school instructor.

JAY, from Pennsylvania, is a geologist, retired from NASA and teaching.

LEE AND KYLE, from Virginia, are father and son. Lee is a high school science teacher. Kyle is an avid reader, hiker, and gamer.

LINDSEY, from Virginia, is an elementary school teacher.

LORRE, from Florida, is a real estate agent.

MARGARET, from Pennsylvania, is an urban gardener and book editor.

ZAHRA, from Ontario, is a specialist in multicultural cuisine.

A Map for Learning How to Freestyle Cook

Gini lays out some groundwork for winging it in the kitchen:

YOU CAN ALSO ASK A FRIEND or two to tell you how they prepare a dish and write down their directions. You won't have a precise recipe, but you may get instructions like "Add flour until it feels right," and you'll have to feel your way through. That process will embed in your memory in a different— and a good—way, letting ingredients lead rather than following a prescriptive recipe.

You have to be passionate, or at the very least *interested*, in food to improvise. —GINI

1. Take a favorite recipe and make it faithfully one night, following each step and ingredient to the letter.

2. The next week, make that same dish using the recipe only as a reference. When you've done this, write a stripped-down version of the method you followed.

3. The following week, try to make the recipe without using your reference, and also substitute a few ingredients. (Encourage the people you may be cooking for to be open to the process of improvisation!)

4. The next time you make the dish, improvise further, adding, subtracting, or substituting ingredients in whatever way inspires you. Make notes about what you did. Keep track of the changes that you liked.

RIGHT: Start with these delicious ingredients (top left) in various amounts and combinations. Turn them into loaded tacos, a pizza, or a bowl.

Good Things to Know

1. Don't cook to impress.

EUGENE SAYS: About 20 years ago, I began to appreciate the way my mom used to cook. Her food wasn't fancy, but she always started with very good ingredients.

As I became less of a food snob, I became more improvisational. My ideas about entertaining changed from "How can I impress everyone?" to "How can we have a good dinner with enjoyable conversation and great food?" Where I once made beef Wellington complete with foie gras, I now make homemade pasta and have a kitchen full of friends helping to roll out and stuff different kinds of ravioli.

2. Keep it simple and be flexible.

ZAHRA SAYS: Recently, we were expecting my in-laws for a visit the next day. I thought they were coming late in the afternoon and that we were going to a restaurant for dinner to celebrate my mother-in-law's birthday. Somehow I was mixed up about the times, only to find out that they were arriving in one hour for a lunch at our house—that I had not planned to prepare!

It was a special occasion, so the meal couldn't seem thoughtless. I was in a panic! *No* time to run to the grocery store. I did a quick scan of the fridge and pantry. I had leftover chicken breast on the bone, some leftover cooked basmati rice, tomatoes, onions, cilantro, chiles, and coconut cream. I decided to make what comes easily to me and always tastes good: curry. What's my point? Keep it simple!

I had almost everything I needed for a Thai yellow curry, except one vital ingredient—lemongrass. I thought it would never be missed if I added extra ginger and turmeric. I needed to be flexible or this dish wasn't going to happen.

I shredded the chicken, popped the onions in the food processor, and started sautéing things like a madwoman. Just as my in-laws arrived, I managed to have the curry bubbling away on the stove as though that had been my plan all along. My mother-in-law loved the meal!

I learned that when I'm in a bind, I'll have a good chance of landing well if I make what I know and am flexible about the ingredients. Curry may seem fancy, but it's what I grew up eating. It's what I know. I've found that making what I know gives me room to experiment because I understand the components of the dish so well that I can be flexible with the ingredients. Beyond being flexible, I can be creative.

So being flexible opens the door to creativity. And special does not always mean fancy!

3. Be organized.

GINI SAYS: If you have a really small kitchen, you can still cook well. Organization is the currency of good cooking, not space!

4. Hold your cooking plans lightly.

CHUCK SAYS: We wanted a salad to go with the split pea soup we were reheating on the stove. There on the counter was a bunch of avocados, a few already soft. I had them on the cutting board, a lime sliced and ready to be squeezed over the avocado to keep it from browning while I figured out the rest of the salad. But as I was about to cut open the avocado, I remembered that we had just picked several bushels of late-fall, half-wormy-but-super-tasty apples off a neglected tree nearby. As we were picking, I'd mentioned Waldorf salad. In the fridge was also celery that needed to be used up, and we had plenty of walnuts in the freezer.

The avocados went into the fridge, and with a bit of quick chopping and a touch of yogurt and mayo, we had a lovely late-fall salad.

I'm trying to become more aware, too, of when to cook and when to take it easy. The dish I have my heart set on may require more time and effort than is wise to give under the circumstances. As much as I love to cook and eat good food, sometimes a relaxed evening with bread and cheese is better than a big production, lots of messy dishes, and going to bed late.

5. Prep in your head.

I need some space to think when I'm cooking our evening meal, so I often create a "first course"—and I'm not talking fancy. That first course is a good-sized platter of cut-up fresh vegetables or fruit slices that I set out for the gathering crowd in the kitchen who are all moaning from hunger. I prep the celery sticks and hummus, or apple slices and yogurt, in the morning while working on breakfast or packing lunches. I offer small plates for this first course to make sure people don't get full before the main meal is ready.

ZAHRA SAYS: I do an inventory of the food I have on hand on my way home from work. My goal is to make a meal plan before I get to the door.

The first question I ask myself is, What do I have that's already cooked and ready to work with? Then I think about food groups, so we have a balanced meal. What protein, vegetables, and starches do I have already prepared—or not yet prepared—that I could build on?

What's in my fridge that ought to be used up? Does it need to be cleaned, chopped, grated, steamed, blanched, or cooked, and how long will that take? What am I craving? What's my family likely to be hungry for?

If I can focus enough to do this inventory gathering as I'm on my way home, I walk in the door ready to go. With practice, the process gets quicker and quicker.

6. Make extra to use later.

MARGARET SAYS: I often do planned leftovers. I just don't call them leftovers. I refer to them as "the base for this evening's meal" or "the roasted veggies" or "the browned beef." And I use different serving bowls for this round.

7. Freeze cooked food in meal-sized portions.

I've finally caught on. I used to freeze a whole batch in a single container, which took hours to thaw and then left us with too much food left over again. Now I save sturdy take-out dishes and their lids and divide my prepped food among them. On the label I note what the dish is, the likely number of servings, and the date when I froze it.

8. Look for cooking inspiration everywhere.

EUGENE SAYS: My inspiration is usually seasonal and ingredient based. I'm inspired by the visual appeal of food. As a former fashion designer, I love color, texture, shape, and contrast. I often Google images for a specific ingredient and look at the pictures instead of reading the recipe. This fall, we found wonderful fresh figs at the grocery store, and I had a big bag of shelled pistachios. I Googled "figs pistachios" and found a great picture of sliced figs with mascarpone cheese sprinkled with pistachios and balsamic vinegar.

I love to improvise with new takes on old standbys, too, such as Mom's meatloaf now made with ground lamb and Indian spices and served with cardamom roasted potatoes.

I'm also inspired to try to cook with a sensibility toward sustainable living. I try to buy local produce and fair-trade products.

I struggle with what I call food elitism. I've made mac and cheese for years with béchamel, grated cheese, and breadcrumb topping. This used to be a frugal dish. Now that I make it with the requisite imported and properly aged cheeses and organic dairy, it costs about $45 for a 4-quart casserole. This bothers me, because people working at minimum wage would need to work nearly 5 hours to make this authentic, sustainable version for their family.

CHUCK SAYS: Even without immediate access to a store, a farm, or a good food truck on the corner, you can usually pull something together. A few Sundays back, we invited a nephew and his wife for lunch after church. We had no idea what we would make, and there wasn't a critical mass of anything in the fridge, only a bit of this and some of that, but we pulled together a salad.

Since I raise both rabbits and chickens and have a garden, my first solution is usually to forage in the garden for whatever greens are in season and to quickly think of what we can make with them. I might notice that we have lots of peppers on hand and the basil needs trimming. I can imagine collecting eggs, picking a few herbs, and making an omelet.

There are some things you should *never* be without—mayonnaise, cans of tuna, onions, and nuts, to name a few. If you have one apple languishing in the back of the fridge, a bit of celery, maybe three pickle slices left in the bottom of a jar, you have a start on an interesting salad.

9. Figure out what makes a good substitute ingredient.

DARYL SAYS: I like experimenting with different flavors, seeing what goes with what and especially choosing a local ingredient whenever I can instead of one that's been shipped. I often use rhubarb, for example, if I need extra acidity and tartness in a dish. A lemon or lime might be the customary ingredient to reach for, but I want to stay local. We grow rhubarb; we don't grow lemons. I keep rhubarb in the freezer for that very reason. Savory meat sauces have turned out to be exceptional when I've made them with rhubarb.

So this is the way I think: Are there other foods that might be a good substitute for the usual ingredient because they add something similar to a dish? What if a dish asks for peppers and I don't have any? Can I skip the peppers? Or is there something else I can use instead?

10. Honor ancient food traditions.

GINI SAYS: It's fun to try to replicate a great dish you ate in a Salvadoran or Korean restaurant, but understand that it may take a while to get it right.

Approach a food tradition that's different from your own with respect. If you want to prepare its dishes authentically, read about it. Take some time to understand it. Choose a recipe from a knowledgeable author. If you attempt

to cook the dish with integrity, you'll likely keep going back to it so you can build on what you've learned.

For example, Western cuisine has been using spices for only 200 years. We lack the expertise compared to Asian and Indian cuisines that have been developing spice blends for thousands of years!

11. Gather a good supply of basic cooking tools.

EUGENE SAYS: In my early days of cooking, I cooked improvisationally for myself, but for guests, I followed a recipe because I was afraid of making mistakes. As I developed a certain amount of skill with cooking techniques, I began to feel more confident and willing to improvise.

Tools like an instant-read meat thermometer make it much easier to improvise, especially with meat, fish, and poultry. I certainly feel freer to improvise because I now have a way to prevent that beautiful fillet of cod from going over 130°F (54°C).

TOOLS FOR EVERY KITCHEN, NO MATTER ITS SIZE

- wooden spoons (2)
- easily pliable, heat-resistant spatulas, 10 to 10½ inches long (2)
- paring knife, chef's knife, and serrated knife
- whisk, 12 inches long
- offset metal spatula with a 1½- to 2-inch-wide blade

- instant-read meat thermometer
- cutting board(s)
- 2-quart glass measuring bowl (microwaveable)
- mixing bowls—three sizes that nest in each other
- heat-resistant colander
- Dutch oven
- 10- or 12-inch cast-iron skillet

- sheet pans (2)
- 9-inch square baking dish with lid, for microwave and oven
- 9- by 13-inch baking pan with lid, for microwave and oven
- containers with tight-fitting lids for storing leftovers
- other tools that any cooks you respect can't live without!

12. Try inviting your guests to cook with you!

If you wish you were relaxed about inviting people over spontaneously, or having drop-in friends stay for dinner, or urging your kids to bring friends home after the game, then you might want to invite them into your kitchen to cook with you.

Learn to feel comfortable with a simple meal. Humans love to eat together. People dropping by is a celebration. Inviting them to stay for a meal and having them accept our busy world is a pleasure—carry that air of celebration into the meal preparation space.

So, what to cook?

GINI SAYS:

- Aim to always have good soup ingredients in your pantry or soup in the freezer. Then invite your guests to help you make a quick biscuit or scone recipe for a delicious, enticing accompaniment.

- If you have canned tomatoes in your pantry, and you have an onion, potatoes or pasta, and cayenne, you're on your way to a spicy tomato soup.

- White beans, garlic, broth/stock/water, parsley, and seasonings can become a white bean soup.

- Cornmeal and water can become polenta, topped with leftover meat and tomato sauce or black beans.

- Make a salad of chickpeas or any canned beans, hard-cooked eggs, and tuna on lettuce, or stir that mixture into cooked pasta.

- Top an already-cooked grain with a sauce or dressing.

13. Be creative with shortages.

ZAHRA SAYS: **When I was a kid,** my mother used to tell us about the time she came up with her famous dish, Sauce Varu Chicken. The name means "chicken with sauce," which makes me laugh because it sounds so boring in English, but we used to request this dish a lot.

She said she was short on ingredients for some reason. All she had was a bit of butter, tomato paste, salt, pepper, and rice. So she started cooking,

using her usual cooking methods, and she ended up making a wonderful chicken dish with a very buttery, peppery tomato sauce. It was so delicious that she kept making it for us, for friends, and for anyone who requested it.

Sauce Varu Chicken is memorable not only because it tasted good, but because she made it on the fly. Unexpected shortages can drive us to be creative.

Sometimes, I create shortages on purpose. Maybe I want to whittle things down in the fridge for a fresh start, or the season is changing, or I'm bored, or I'm going on a trip. Halting grocery shopping means I've got to be creative.

It can be a little scary, but I'm always surprised by how resourceful I can be. I love the process because, inevitably, I find things in the fridge, freezer, or pantry that I've forgotten, but they're still good and need to be eaten.

My brain also gets a workout trying to orchestrate something complementary out of random ingredients. Sometimes the meals are disjointed—the dishes don't match each other culturally, but that's okay. I think of it as a potluck. The individual elements are delicious, and harmony is sometimes overrated.

In the end, I begin a new cooking season with a nearly blank slate and a lot of ideas.

14. Invite a child to help you cook.

LORRE SAYS: I learned to cook from my grandmothers and my mother because I was welcome in their kitchens. My mom was the best at telling me what she was doing and why. She still offers little tips that make a difference in the outcome of a dish.

Welcoming children into the kitchen is a great practice of patience, but it is a beautiful gift they are likely to hand down to their children.

That's how I learned not to be afraid to try all kinds of cooking experiments. Lucky me.

15. Handle your food wisely.

BETH SAYS: Treat ingredients like they're going to nourish you. Handle them kindly. Plan. Prepare. Present. The visual is part of eating, too.

You know, the more you have to do with food, the more it gives back—to the cook and to those who eat it.

Ingredients to Have on Hand

Since everyone has different food preferences, it doesn't make much sense to follow a generic list about which ingredients to always have on hand. Instead, start with what you like to eat and make and what the people you usually cook for like to eat.

Create two lists:

1. Flavors you and your household like

2. Ingredients you enjoy that can be cooked easily and are wholesome and delicious

Think, too, about your various storage places—fridge, cupboard or pantry, and maybe a freezer—and what you'll put where. For example, if you like to eat seasonally, there's a lot of happy coming and going in your fridge, and maybe your freezer, too, especially during the growing season. But things go best if you also keep a supply of complementary ingredients on hand. And you'll be less likely to panic about mealtime if you always have backup ingredients, particularly when your fresh produce supply is a little thin or out of balance.

Essential Ingredient Hints from the Cooking Circle

ZAHRA SAYS: **If I had to name one thing** that helps me the most in any cooking situation, it's having certain ingredients on hand as much as possible. But before I gather any of these items, I figure out the flavors I tend to seek out in my food. That affects what I keep in my spice cabinet, pantry, fridge, and freezer. I always have the spices I use the most, as well as their refills stored away for easy top-ups.

I aim to keep "malleable" ingredients in all those places, too. For example, I always have red lentils, rice, and coconut milk in the pantry. The lentils do not need to be soaked overnight and cook up fairly quickly. Rice goes with many things. Coconut milk adds a creamy and sweet dimension to many dishes.

- almond milk
- balsamic vinegar
- bread-and-butter pickles (they make the best tartar sauce!)
- bread flour
- broth, or at the very least bouillon
- butter
- canned fish (clams, anchovies, tuna)
- cumin
- double-smoked bacon
- eggs
- fresh parsley and thyme
- gluten-free baking mix
- good vinegars (an assortment)
- herbes de Provence
- lemons
- mustard
- oils (an assortment)
- olives
- panko
- salsa
- salt
- tomato sauce
- veal stock
- yeast

My fridge always has a jar of puréed ginger and a jar of puréed garlic because they're called for in so many of my dishes. I also tend to keep a lot of root vegetables in storage because they last a long time and can be used in many different ways.

EVONNE SAYS: I try to keep a variety of fresh foods on hand, including mixed greens, cauliflower, bell peppers, onions, garlic, tomatoes (in season), spinach, lettuce, mushrooms, celery, carrots, sweet and white potatoes, green beans, broccoli, and tofu. We have a garden, so in summer, I shop to supplement what's growing at the moment.

My pantry has canned coconut milk, canned tomatoes, sun-dried tomatoes, pasta, rice, quinoa, couscous, lentils, emergency canned black beans and chickpeas (in case I run out of frozen ones that I cook from dried), raw cashews, and other nuts.

My freezer has broccoli, corn, green beans, peas, applesauce, edamame, mixed mushrooms, cooked black beans, cooked chickpeas, mixed berries, chopped mangoes, sliced peaches, and a mix of edamame, corn, and red bell peppers.

If you have to substitute for fresh, go with your personal preference, whether that's frozen or canned. For example, I would rather use canned diced tomatoes than "fresh" out-of-season tomatoes.

I like to have a variety of spices available so I can keep discovering new combinations that my family likes, and, of course, continue making what we already enjoy. Spices make a huge difference in the tastes of food. They do lose their flavor, so if you have access to a local spice or bulk food store, buy a small amount of a variety of spices for lots of options with flavors at their peak.

Whenever I grocery shop, I restock any of these items we're running low on.

LEE SAYS: We have a big garden, and I love to can, so that's reflected in what we always have on hand.

For fruits, we keep canned peaches and applesauce as well as frozen blueberries and strawberries.

For vegetables, we freeze green beans, peas, broccoli, and corn, and we keep either fresh-from-the-garden or winter-stored potatoes, onions, sweet potatoes, and squash. We have greens when they're in season.

For meat, I can chicken (the breast, legs, and wings of one soup hen fit into a quart jar most of the time!) and cubed venison. We have begun butchering our own pork and chicken. We raise beef as well and pay a butcher to cut up a quarter or half, depending on how much of the beef we sell. (I no longer buy meat I can raise.) One part I like about butchering is that it encourages me to be resourceful and find delicious ways to use nonprime cuts.

We keep a wide variety of grains and flours on hand, as well as dried beans and rice.

Cooking without Wasting

It takes some deliberation to cook only what you intend to eat (including leftovers), but it's not really that hard. In fact, why not allot part of your cooking creativity and inspiration to not wasting food?

We who live where food is abundant, near gardens and fields of vegetables and fruits, feel little direct consequence when we let food spoil or fill our plates with more than we can eat.

We all know how easy it is to be too enthusiastic and overbuy fresh food. But we're now recognizing how our planet suffers when we blithely send brown, soft food down the garbage disposal or put it out in the trash. So why don't we each decide to begin a composting project alongside our increased freestyle cooking? Make them partner efforts. Develop a conscience about it. We know we'll have some waste now and then, so we can set up a solution before it happens. It's just another way to respect the ingredients we plan to use—and their soil source. Treating food with respect is an important aspect of freestyle cooking.

Waste-Less Hints from the Cooking Circle

EVONNE SAYS: Before I start making our evening meal, I check for any food that doesn't have many days left. I make sure to use it, either by incorporating it or creating an entirely new dish around it.

***

DARYL SAYS: We live in the center of a city, but we keep a rather large compost bin outside and a worm composting box in our basement. Any nonmeat food that has become the victim of our poor planning and has spent too long in our refrigerator gets tossed into one of those places.

Old food that gets transformed into rich dirt that fertilizes our plants isn't really wasted, right? Especially if we put it onto strawberry beds or the herb garden or around the fig tree where it eventually turns into fresh food. Or if it gives a nutritional boost to the indoor plants that freshen our breathing air and boost our spirits as they grow all around us. Please say that's not wasted food.

I have learned the value of making a menu before going shopping and buying only what I need for the menu. That helps me be careful about spur-of-the-moment, "Oh, that looks really good" purchases that I don't know what I'll do with. I hate to get home and realize, as I'm putting those good-looking veggies into the fridge, that I won't have any time in the coming week to cook what I just bought. Sticking to a menu as I'm shopping helps, as does going to the grocery store with a full stomach.

In our household, we make ample use of our freezer. If a dish looks like it's going to sit too long in the fridge, we label it, move it to the freezer, and have a ready-made meal to eat when we need it.

We also spread out some food on a baking sheet and freeze it. When it's frozen, we pull it off the sheet, put it in a freezer container with a secure lid, label it, and return it, still frozen, to the freezer. We do this with bacon, which my spouse and I both love. We consider bacon an accent food; a small amount gives us the spark of flavor that we want. A whole pound will spoil in the time it takes us to eat it, so we pull it apart and freeze it as individual pieces that we can easily take out one piece at a time.

We make big batches of beans in an electric pressure cooker and freeze them in meal-sized amounts that we can thaw as needed. Not only is that convenient, but it also prevents excess beans from going to waste.

CHRISTINA SAYS: It is so easy to be too enthusiastic and overbuy fresh food. If I do this (and it happens more than I like to admit), I aim to make meals for the rest of the week and store them in the fridge. Or I invite people over when I have too much and just share it all. It's a great excuse for a dinner party.

I try to be inspired, too, by how generations before us did it. My grandmother canned or froze all kinds of vegetables and fruit. If I overbuy fresh corn in summer, I channel my grandma: boil all the corn, shave it off the cob, and freeze it. Channeling your inner grandma is not a bad thing.

I make extra tomatoes into sauce with fresh basil and freeze that for another time. With blueberries, I simply stick them in a freezer-safe container and then into the freezer as is. Or, if I have extra time, I make them into jam. I purée fresh peaches, put them in the freezer, and add them to my yogurt in fall and winter. Most of these ideas are recycled from another generation, but that's because they work!

EUGENE SAYS: Because I live alone, I constantly feel guilty whenever fresh fruits and vegetables begin to wilt, so now I buy ziplock bags of frozen mixed fruit, such as mangoes, peaches, and strawberries. When I have small amounts of extra fresh fruit (grapes, strawberries, blueberries), I toss them into the bag with the other frozen fruit. Frozen grapes are great in a glass of wine!

I make chicken stock sometimes in a slow cooker, and then I'm glad for ribs of celery and other vegetables. I should keep a ziplock bag in the freezer for ingredients for stock, such as leftover vegetables and wilted produce (note to self).

ZAHRA SAYS: Sometimes I sauté vegetables that seem like they're on their way out—parsnips, chard, onions, celery, carrots, mushrooms, anything really. When they're in that state, they're better suited to cooking than to eating fresh.

JAY SAYS: When zucchinis won't stop growing, make a few batches of zucchini lasagna. Eat one and freeze the rest. You'll be ready for more of the big Z by December.

When grape or cherry tomatoes arrive by the busload, sauté them in a little olive oil and freeze. They're easy to use all winter long in soups and Italian dishes, spread over toast, or by themselves.

FROM GINI:
Three Waste-Less Approaches to Try

1. Make dishes with five or fewer ingredients. It's a helpful way to keep your fridge free of an ingredient you're not likely to use again. Shop three or four times a week for only the items you've planned for.

2. Commit to being willing to eat leftovers.

3. Find others who share your commitment and practice. Then get together now and then to make and share good food.

BETH SAYS: When some of my potatoes develop brown spots, I rescue them by chunking the potatoes (getting rid of the brown spots as I go along) and roasting the good parts with hot sausage for a full meal. They are soooo good. Why would I throw them out? Food is healing, after all!

GINI SAYS: I don't force myself to use all of the dandelion greens if I get an unmanageable amount in my CSA box. I let myself off the hook if eating something is going to be unpleasant. I am careful about quantity and buy fresh things a few times a week. Then I'm less likely to let them stockpile in the fridge and go bad.

MARGARET SAYS: If I have a mistake or failure, I alter it if I can think of a good way to do that. Making a puréed soup is a great trick, depending on what the problem was.

Making the Most of Simple Ingredients

While on a 20-day walk from Kitchener to Ottawa one spring, I had an opportunity to do some free-style cooking. Our hosts along the way would often lay out a potluck-style meal for us, which we were very thankful for after our daily 18-mile journey. One night near Toronto, our hosts provided the ingredients for our dinner but left the cooking to us.

I arrived early to make the meal before the rest of the walkers got there. I found potatoes, chicken, and a few seasoning ingredients, so the cooking methods became really important. I pounded the chicken and seasoned it with salt and pepper. Next I dredged it in flour, then egg, and finally breadcrumbs. I used paprika and garlic as extra seasoning, and then I fried the meat on high heat for about 1 minute per side. This produced delightfully crispy, schnitzel-like chicken. I served it with mashed potatoes—and I used a lot of butter!

This was definitely a simple meal, yet the satisfying contrasts in texture made up for the lack of diverse ingredients. I was able to love the ingredients into something more than just chicken and potatoes! Many walkers commented that this was one of their favorite meals.

I keep my home pantry stocked with homemade pesto, tomato sauce, olive oil, olives, lemons, canned artichokes, sun-dried tomatoes, canned clams, and tuna. I can make any number of combinations of fresh pasta and sauces, which are simple and easy but also high-quality. Often, it is the pairing of a few good items that becomes the heart of a meal—rather than a recipe!

1 / VEGETABLES

IT'S EASY TO MAKE VEGETABLES the starting point of your meal at least two or three times a week. How? Let's say you've decided to make a frittata for one of your meals. As you out up vegetables for it, keep chunking and chopping until you have enough for a pasta sauce and also a soup later in the week. Now you have a start on three meals.

Looking for inspiration? Think about plant-based dishes eaten around the world. In Asia, there are curries, spiced chickpeas, and seasoned potatoes. In the Mediterranean, you find eggplant, hummus, falafel, tomatoes, cucumbers, and gazpacho. In Latin America, rice and beans, pozole, salsa, squash, tomatoes, avocados, chiles, and corn are featured.

If you're still not sure what to make:

- **Figure out which cooking method**—steaming? sautéing? roasting?—will bring out the most flavor from your vegetables.

- **Consider the time you have to cook.** Sautéing, steaming, and microwaving are handy when you have limited time. Roasting and braising are best if you get home early and have some extra time, as they take little tending.

- **Follow the colors.** The more colorful the vegetables, the more nutritious. Think rainbow both when you shop for vegetables and when you cook so you can serve colorful—and healthy—plates of food.

Best Vegetable Cooking Methods

VEGETABLES	SAUTÉ (p. 37)	ROAST/BAKE (p. 40)	STIR-FRY (p. 45)	BRAISE (p. 50)	STEAM (p. 53)	MICROWAVE (p. 55)	GRILL (p. 56)
asparagus	x	x	x		x	x	x
beets		x		x		x	x
broccoli	x	x	x		x	x	x
Brussels sprouts	x	x	x		x	x	x
cabbage	x	x	x	x	x	x	x
carrots	x	x	x	x	x	x	x
cauliflower	x	x	x		x	x	x
corn	x	x			x	x	x
eggplant	x	x	x			x	x
green beans	x	x	x	x	x	x	
kale	x	x			x	x	
mushrooms	x		x		x	x	x
onions	x	x	x	x		x	x
peppers	x		x			x	x
potatoes (white and sweet)	x	x		x	x	x	x
snow peas	x		x		x	x	x
spinach	x				x	x	
sugar snap peas	x		x		x	x	
summer squash	x	x	x		x	x	x
Swiss chard	x				x	x	
tomatoes	x	x			x	x	x
winter squash		x	x	x	x	x	
zucchini	x	x	x		x	x	x

35
vegetables

Add an acid such as vinegar to bitter greens like kale to help neutralize their strong flavor.

SAUTÉING

Advantages: It's quick and it concentrates the flavor.

BEST VEGETABLES FOR SAUTÉING

- **Brussels sprouts** (halved)
- **cabbage** (chopped)
- **carrots** (diced)
- **cauliflower and broccoli florets** (chopped)
- **corn kernels**
- **grape or cherry tomatoes**
- **green beans**
- **onions, mushrooms, and zucchini** (sliced)
- **potatoes** (white and sweet; diced)
- **spinach and kale** (chopped)
- **sugar snap peas**

HINTS

- **Don't crowd the skillet.** The vegetables should fit on the bottom of the skillet in one layer with some space between the pieces. That allows each piece direct contact with the skillet so it can brown and caramelize. If the skillet's too full, the veggies will just steam in their own juices. If you have a small skillet or lots of vegetables, sauté in batches for the best results.
- **Acid and bitter neutralize each other.** You can add acid in the form of lemon juice or apple cider vinegar to things like dandelion greens, kale, and collards when sautéing or wilting them to counter their natural bitterness. Consider adding a good amount of butter, too, and season them well with salt and pepper to keep the flavors melded and smooth. —GINI
- **Add a splash of apple cider vinegar** to the vegetables as you sauté them to add a light kick to a dish without overpowering other flavors. You can use balsamic vinegar as well, but be more careful because balsamic vinegar is sweeter than apple cider vinegar and has a more potent flavor. —LINDSEY

STEPS TO TAKE

1. **Heat a skillet** over medium-high heat.

2. **Add oil and/or butter** slowly so it doesn't splatter. A mix of the two is good; the oil keeps the butter from burning, and the butter brings flavor.

3. **Add the veggies immediately** when the oil/butter is hot and/or melted.

4. **Stir now and then** so the vegetables don't burn or overcook.

5. **Turn off the burner** when the veggies are just softened (this takes only a few minutes) and remove the skillet from the heat.

6. **Season (or not)** and eat as soon as possible.

What's the Difference between Sautéing, Stir-Frying, and Braising?

Sautéing and stir-frying are both quick-cooking methods. Braising is a longer cooking process.

Sautéing is done over medium heat in just a bit of fat—either oil or butter, or a combination of the two. The intent is to lightly brown the food on each side, which usually takes a few minutes. It may require longer cooking to cook through.

Stir-frying is done over high heat in oil (butter would burn) and requires the food to be moved continually so it doesn't burn or scorch. Food that will be stir-fried should be cut into thin, relatively small pieces so it can be easily flipped from side to side. It cooks quickly and should be removed from the hot skillet as soon as it's done.

Braising is done in liquid on the stovetop or in the oven. It works well for meats that need extended cooking over low heat or for vegetables that become soft and silky but keep their flavor after long cooking. Braising usually begins with sautéing. Once the food is browned, it goes into a Dutch oven, stockpot, or roasting pan. Enough well-seasoned broth is added to half cover the food. Then the pot is covered and the food cooks gently over low to medium heat, often for 2 to 3 hours.

DRESSING UP SAUTÉED VEGETABLES

- **Spoon melted or browned butter,** or flavored nut oils, over freshly sautéed vegetables just before serving.

- **Have fresh spinach that's about to bite the dust?** Sauté it with some garlic oil and basil. Always finish by adding a dash of ground nutmeg to spinach. —LORRE

- **Sautéed cabbage is versatile.** Depending on what else you're eating, you can add fennel, tomatoes, and garlic to tilt the cabbage Italian; mix in cilantro, sesame oil, and peanuts to make it Vietnamese or Thai; or toss in carrots and scallions to move it toward Chinese. Or keep the basic recipe, sautéing the cabbage with onions and lemon juice and serving it alongside almost anything. —MARGARET

STORIES FROM THE COOKING CIRCLE: **CHUCK**
You Can Sauté That?!

A brewer friend mentioned that you can eat hops shoots. I've been growing Cascade hops around our house for a number of years now, but nobody had ever told me hops could be served as a meal! So I went out and picked a bunch of shoots. I threw them into a skillet with a bit of butter and salt and did a quick sauté. I had a nice blue cheese sitting on the cutting board, so I grabbed a nibble of the cheese plus a shoot out of the skillet and decided that combination could work.

I had a little jar of rabbit liver pâté, still sealed under its layer of butter, in the fridge that needed be used. I added that to the table, along with a few glasses of Chardonnay left over in a bottle in the fridge.

So there you have it—an amazingly good and quick supper. The cooked hops shoots were somewhere between asparagus and spinach, and the blue cheese paired perfectly with them.

ROASTING OR BAKING

BEST VEGETABLES FOR ROASTING

- **asparagus spears** (whole or cut on the bias)
- **beets** (whole or chunked)
- **Brussels sprouts** (whole if small; halved if larger)
- **carrots and parsnips** (sliced or cut on the bias)
- **cauliflower and broccoli florets and stems** (peeled and cut into chunks)
- **eggplant** (peeled or not, sliced)
- **green beans**
- **onions and leeks** (sliced thick or chunked)
- **potatoes** (white and sweet; peeled or not, sliced or chunked)
- **tomatoes** (grape or cherry, whole; plum, halved or quartered)
- **winter squash** (peeled and sliced)
- **zucchini and yellow squash** (cut on the bias)

Advantages: It offers matchless flavor! And it doesn't need a lot of stirring or attention.

STEPS TO TAKE

1. **Preheat the oven** to 425°F (220°C) for dense root vegetables or 450°F (230°C) for sturdy green vegetables and veggies with a fairly high moisture content (such as zucchini and eggplant).

2. **Grease** the bottom of a sheet pan or roasting pan well, or cover it with parchment paper.

3. **Cut up the vegetables** but keep the pieces large enough so they're recognizable and keep their identity, flavor-wise.

4. **Mix the vegetables** with olive oil, salt, and freshly ground black pepper.

5. **Scatter the pieces** across the prepared pan in one layer. There is no need to add liquid.

6. **Brush the vegetables** with balsamic or apple cider vinegar for extra flavoring and to encourage caramelization, if desired.

7. **Roast dense root vegetables** for 30 to 60 minutes, depending on the size and number of pieces. For sturdy green vegetables, roast for 15 to 30 minutes, depending on the vegetables and the size and number of pieces. For vegetables with a fairly high moisture content, roast for 5 to 15 minutes, depending on the vegetables and the size and number of pieces.

Instructions continue on page 42

KEEP VEGETABLE "BASICS" AROUND ALL THE TIME. My basics are mushrooms, onions, garlic, tomatoes, spinach, lettuce, white and sweet potatoes, cauliflower, carrots, celery, and bell peppers (red, yellow, and orange). And that's not an exhaustive list. I've also got lots of different grains, rice, flours, nuts, beans and lentils, tofu, and spices in my pantry, fridge, and freezer because most kinds of rice and grains are easy to combine with just about any vegetable dish. —EVONNE

Slice or julienne summer squash and roast it along with chopped red and green bell pepper. Together they develop a great sauce and can be served over cooked rice. —BETH

8. **Keep an eye on things,** especially when you're roasting less-dense vegetables that cook more quickly, so that the vegetables roast but don't shrivel or burn. After the veggies are browned on their bottom side and almost tender, flip them over and continue roasting for another 10 minutes or so, until the second side browns and caramelizes and the vegetables have tender centers.

9. **Taste before serving.** Season or not. Rosemary is good. Consider adding a spoonful of lemon juice, lime juice, or vinegar. Test these ideas first by adding just a bit in the corner of the pan and tasting. Add more if the seasoning works.

10. **Eat as is,** or add the veggies to couscous or a sauce, or use them as a topping on a salad, pizza, bowl, pasta, or toast. Or let them cool and save them for another meal.

TIPS FROM THE COOKING CIRCLE
MAKING THE MOST OF ROASTED OR BAKED VEGETABLES

- **Run a whole scrubbed and trimmed sweet potato** through a spiralizer. Lay the noodles out on a baking sheet. Spray with oil and season. Roast until tender, about 10 minutes at 425°F (220°C). Eat as is or serve mixed with or alongside ground turkey and vegetables, maybe topped with a creamy or marinara sauce.

- **Roast or braise fresh tomatoes.** Frozen tomato sauce is gold. Make a huge batch of it when tomatoes are plentiful so you have it for topping spaghetti, as pizza sauce, in huevos rancheros (eggs poached in tomato sauce), and for a host of other dishes. Keep the seasoning minimal so you can simply thaw the tomato sauce and use it in any dish without it being a mismatch. —DARYL

- **Always roast four or five extra potatoes.** Add more russet, yellow, or red-skinned potatoes to the oven than you need for that evening's dinner. Turn them into fried potatoes with eggs the next morning or evening. Yellow and red potatoes fry well. —BETH

My Roasting Rhythm

I tend to roast a sheet pan or two full of mixed veggies once each week to have them on hand for topping salads and pasta, to eat as a side dish, or to toss in omelets and quiches. And to pack in my lunch. They reheat well and are tasty warm or cold.

The great thing about roasted vegetables is that the quantity of each isn't important. Only have half a carrot left over? Great—throw it in. A quarter of a red onion that needs to be used? Perfect! You can literally use whatever you have.

The only caveat is minding the rate at which each vegetable will cook. If you have a lot of root vegetables in the mix, hold the broccoli and cauliflower back for the first 20 minutes, then toss them in.

Vary the seasonings depending on what you're in the mood for. Toss roasted vegetables in a little oil and vinegar, add your favorite spices and herbs, and you've got a healthy, versatile, and delicious addition to any meal.

Some of my favorite seasoning combinations are:

- cumin, chili powder, and cilantro
- curry powder and red pepper flakes
- dill and lemon juice
- basil, oregano, and garlic powder

Add vegetables that need the longest cooking time first.

To add interesting texture, top stir-fried vegetables with uncooked corn kernels, sliced fresh mushrooms, and/or a chiffonade of fresh spinach, chard, kale, water-cress, or arugula.

ESSENTIAL TECHNIQUE
STIR-FRYING

Advantages: It's fast and results in somewhat crispy vegetables with highly concentrated flavor.

BEST VEGETABLES FOR STIR-FRYING

- **asparagus and carrots** (cut on the bias)
- **bell peppers** (diced)
- **Brussels sprouts** (halved, depending on their size)
- **cauliflower and broccoli florets and stems** (peeled and cut into small chunks)
- **corn kernels**
- **fresh herbs** (chopped)
- **green beans**
- **mushrooms** (sliced)
- **onions** (sliced)
- **snow peas**
- **sprouts**
- **winter squash** (peeled and sliced)
- **zucchini and yellow squash** (chunked)

CUTTING VEGGIES ON THE BIAS means that more of each piece will be in contact with the hot bottom of the skillet.

STEPS TO TAKE

1. **Prep all the vegetables first,** cutting them to size so they're ready when you need them. It's best to slice them thin so the intense heat penetrates the individual pieces while you stir them. You won't have time to stop once you start stir-frying without sacrificing the texture of the vegetables in the hot pan.

2. **Heat the skillet** over high heat.

3. **Add 1 to 2 tablespoons** vegetable or peanut oil, which can withstand high heat, when the skillet is hot. Butter is likely to burn because of the constantly high temperature.

4. **Add the densest veggies** that need the longest cooking time first: onions, green beans, broccoli, cauliflower, Brussels sprouts, carrots, and winter squash. Cook until they soften and blister, stirring constantly so they don't stick or burn.

5. **Add the next-dense vegetables**—zucchini and yellow squash, asparagus, and mushrooms—and continue stirring. Cook just until they soften slightly and begin to brighten in color.

6. **Add the more delicate vegetables**—corn kernels, bell peppers, sprouts, fresh herbs—and continue to stir everything together. Cook until the vegetables are slightly crunchy but still brightly colored. Do not overcook.

7. **Stir in any seasonings,** sauce, or eggs, and heat through to coat the vegetables.

8. **Serve immediately** over your choice of base—rice, wheat berries, farro, quinoa, or pasta.

WHAT TO DO WITH LEFTOVER VEGGIES

Gini shared these great ideas:

- **Add grated carrots** to cooked (or uncooked) breakfast cereal, along with a shake or two of ground cardamom and almond or regular milk.

- **Serve slow-roasted tomatoes** as a side. They are particularly delicious with baked macaroni and cheese.

- **Roast bell peppers** and preserve them in oil to be used on pizza, in salads, and over pasta.

- **Make a slaw,** kraut, or kimchi with leftover cabbage.

- **Put together a pot pie** with leftover vegetables.

VEGGIE STAND-INS

- **Use sliced sweet potatoes and eggplant,** or just long ribbons of zucchini, in place of noodles when making lasagna. —GINI

Lorre shared these great ideas:

- **Use cauliflower instead of grits** in shrimp 'n' grits. Chop it fine or use a food processor. Cook the pieces in a *tiny* bit of chicken broth—the cauliflower gives off lots of moisture, so you only need to steam it a bit. Add some fresh grated nutmeg, and season with salt and pepper to taste.

- **Mashed cauliflower** is an excellent substitute for mashed potatoes. Chop a full head, steam the pieces, and mash them. Stir in minced garlic or garlic powder, a dash of ground nutmeg, and salt and pepper.

Sauté lettuce if it's starting to wilt, and add other vegetables you may or may not usually cook, such as sugar snap peas, celery, or radishes.

STIR-FRY SAUCE

Bring surprising flavor to your stir-fry with a light, savory-sweet sauce.
Go easy on the amount of oil and honey. Go modest on the amount of soy
sauce and fruit juice. Taste. Swirl in some more juice for a brighter flavor.

1. **Pour lightly flavorful sesame oil or avocado oil** into a small skillet.
   Stir in pressed fresh ginger and let it soften a bit over medium heat.
   Then stir in pressed garlic to soften, too.

2. **Add orange juice or coconut water,** soy sauce, and honey. Stir until
   the sauce is well mixed and beginning to simmer around the edges.

3. **To thicken the sauce,** if desired, combine 1 part arrowroot starch with
   2 parts cool water in a small bowl. When the starch has dissolved, stir
   the mixture into the simmering sauce with a whisk just until it thickens.
   Then take the sauce off the heat.

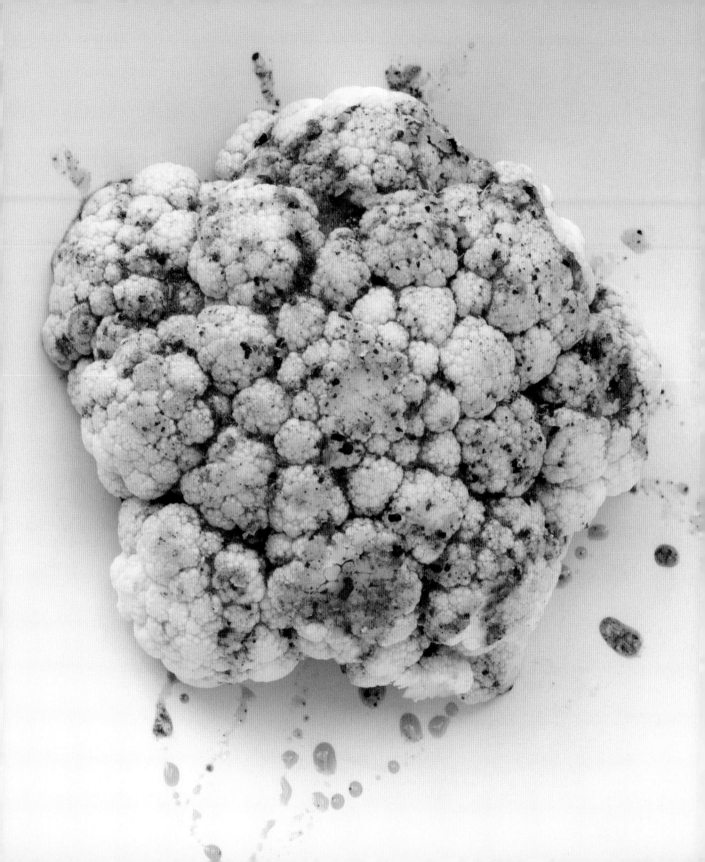

BRAISING

Advantages: It offers a melty outcome in a silky sauce. When done right, the vegetables keep their flavor but turn soft. It doesn't require a lot of tending while cooking.

BEST VEGETABLES FOR BRAISING

- beets
- bok choy
- butternut and acorn squash
- cabbage (red or green; sliced)
- carrots
- green beans
- kale
- leeks
- potatoes (white and sweet)
- Swiss chard

STEPS TO TAKE

1. **Decide if you want to flavor** the main vegetable(s) with a mix of minced onion, carrots, and celery, softened or browned in butter and oil. Chop and sizzle them in the pan if you do. Or just add butter and oil to a large pan and heat until melted. Or brown bacon until crispy; then remove the bacon pieces (save for topping the vegetables later, or munch on them while prepping things), but keep the drippings in the pan to flavor the vegetables you'll be braising.

2. **Add the vegetables for braising,** cut into pieces of equal size.

3. **Stir in enough liquid** (broth, stock, wine, lemon or orange juice, or water) to cover the vegetables by 1½ inches.

4. **Bring the mixture to a boil,** then reduce the heat to a simmer and cover. Cook on the stovetop or in a 350°F (180°C) oven until the vegetables are tender, even slightly limp, but haven't disintegrated, about 30 minutes. It could take longer depending on the quantity and size of the veggie pieces.

5. **Use tongs** or a slotted spoon to lift out the braised vegetables and transfer to a serving dish.

6. **Cook the remaining liquid,** uncovered, until it reduces to about half. Season to taste as needed. Consider adding grated ginger, lime juice, or balsamic vinegar.

7. **Add butter or cream** if you want to make the sauce more silky. Pour it over the braised vegetables and serve. You might want to top the dish with red pepper flakes, mint leaves, or crumbled feta cheese.

Steam carrots, then sprinkle them with brown sugar and stir until it melts. Add a dash of orange juice, a pinch of dill, and a scattering of raisins and serve hot. Or stir unseasoned cooked carrots into a curry sauce and serve that over rice. —BETH

Be sure the vegetables are not sitting in the water.

Check for doneness with the tip of a knife.

Don't crowd the pot.

STEAMING

Advantages: It keeps the vegetables' full flavor, color, and nutritional value. It's quick; no fancy instruments required.

BEST VEGETABLES FOR STEAMING

- asparagus
- broccoli
- **Brussels sprouts**
- carrots
- **cauliflower**
- **fresh spinach**
- **green beans**
- **mushrooms**
- **potatoes** (white and sweet)
- **squash** (summer and winter)
- **sugar snap peas**

STEPS TO TAKE

1. **Cut the vegetables into pieces** of about the same size.

2. **Double-check that your steamer basket** or metal colander will fit into the stockpot and that the bottom of the basket will be at least 2½ inches above the floor of the stockpot. (The vegetables should not sit in the water.) If the basket's legs are too short, elevate them by making three or four bunched-up balls of foil, each about 3 inches in diameter. Make sure the basket sits flat and steadily on the balls without touching the water.

3. **Add 1 to 1½ inches of water** to the stockpot. Bring it to a boil.

4. **Place the vegetables** in the basket. If you have lots, don't pack them in. Instead, cook two or more batches so all the veggies benefit equally from the steam. Cover the pot.

5. **Reduce the heat** so the water simmers but doesn't boil. Watch the time and your pot. Use a timer if you have a lot going on. Depending on the size of the chunks and the amount of vegetables in the steamer, asparagus will take about 3 minutes, broccoli about 5 minutes, and carrots about 7 minutes. Use that as a rough guide for similar vegetables.

6. **Slide the point of a paring knife** into the center of a vegetable. If that's easy to do, the vegetables are done.

7. **Decide how much** you want to season and sauce the steamed vegetables and compete with their pure tastes. Steaming vegetables lets their true flavors sing.

HANG ON TO THAT PORTOBELLO BROTH.
Steam or sauté portobellos till they soften. Pour their tasty broth over cooked white rice. It's rich, almost like Worcestershire sauce.
—BETH

HOW TO MAKE THE MOST OF STEAMED VEGETABLES

- **Steam a ton of fresh spinach,** then add browned butter, freshly ground black pepper, and two soft-boiled eggs on top for a fantastic meal.

- **Steam asparagus and winter squash** to soften them just a bit instead of roasting them, which can obliterate their flavor. Mix these lightly softened vegetables in with the heartier roasted ones and serve them all on a big platter.

- **Steam purple potatoes** (they're great in autumn salads) so they keep their color and don't get overlooked among the roasted white potatoes.

- **Steamed vegetables** look beautiful when laid out on a sheet pan or good-looking platter and served with picks. Or mix them gently in a large bowl where their shapes and colors are visible. Top with minced fresh garlic, if you wish. Or serve the vegetables over white rice.

STORIES FROM THE COOKING CIRCLE: **DARYL**

Dried Bean Wonders

I regularly cook a big batch of dried beans, put the plump cooked ones into pint-sized freezer boxes, and freeze them until I'm ready for them—usually as soon as I've emptied the last box from an earlier batch. In effect, I chain-eat frozen beans.

Making them myself means they have the flavors I like, including a lot less salt than supermarket canned beans. So by freezing the beans I cook, I basically have my own convenience food. Of course, I always enjoy those articles claiming that beans are a common ingredient in the diets of those cultures where people live longer than most.

You have a wide choice of dried beans to choose from. Try a bunch of different kinds and see which ones you think are worth freezing. I prefer the texture of small red beans, black beans, and Central American beans. I use them in recipes that call for other beans, and they work well.

MICROWAVING

Advantages: It's relatively fast and preserves the color, nutritional value, and shapes and textures of vegetables—if you don't overcook them. And it saves a pan since you can cook in the serving dish.

**BEST
VEGETABLES
FOR
MICROWAVING**

- **any and all vegetables** that you typically eat cooked

MICROWAVE A POTATO and use it as the base for almost anything. Reheat left-over vegetables, spoon them over the split-open potato, add grated cheese that's been drifting around the fridge, and top with a freshly poached or sunny-side up egg.

My grandmother used leftover mashed potatoes as a fast take on latkes the next day, making them into patties by stir-ring in an egg, slivered scallions, salt, and pepper. She'd bread the little guys, fry them, and serve them with sour cream or applesauce. Yum.

—CHRISTINA

STEPS TO TAKE

1. **If you're starting with raw vegetables,** cut them into uniform-sized pieces and place them in a microwaveable dish that fits into your microwave.
   If you're starting with frozen vegetables that are already cut up, pour them straight into the dish.

2. **Add 2 to 4 tablespoons of water** (depending on the quantity of vegetables) so that the vegetables will steam while cooking. Cover tightly.

3. **Cook the vegetables on high.** Vegetables with a dense texture need 2 to 4 minutes; less dense vegetables will need less time. Stir, moving the vegetables from the side into the center, and those on the bottom up on top.

4. **Cover and continue cooking** for 1 to 4 minutes longer, depending on how tender you want the veggies to be.

5. **Remove the dish from the microwave** when the vegetables are nearly tender and let them stand, covered, for about 2 minutes as they continue to cook in the residual heat.

6. **Lift the cover away from yourself** so you don't get hit with steam. Season the vegetables as you like and serve.

GRILLING

Advantages: It offers a quick cooking time and matchless flavor. And it's easy to add vegetables to the grill when you're grilling meat.

BEST VEGETABLES FOR GRILLING

- **asparagus** (whole or sliced)
- **broccoli** (keep florets attached to the stems)
- **carrots** (sliced)
- **cauliflower** (cut head into ½-inch-thick steaks)
- **corn** (grill in the husk until the kernels caramelize)
- **eggplant** (sliced)
- **mushrooms** (whole or sliced)
- **onions** (sliced)
- **peppers** (bell and hot; whole or sliced)
- **potatoes** (white and sweet)
- **zucchini** (sliced)

STEPS TO TAKE

1. **Preheat the grill** to 350°F to 450°F (180°C to 230°C), or preheat a grill pan until it sizzles when splashed with drops of water.

2. **Slice the vegetables** about ½ inch thick. (Note: To speed up the cooking time of denser vegetables like carrots, you can precook them for a few minutes.)

3. **Sprinkle with salt and pepper,** and drizzle the vegetables with olive oil.

4. **Place the vegetables on the grill** without overlapping the pieces. Lay slices and steaks across the grate so they don't fall through.

5. **Cover the grill.** Cook for 3 to 5 minutes.

6. **Flip everything.**

7. **Grill for another minute, or up to several minutes,** depending on the vegetables.

8. **Transfer the vegetables** to a serving platter when they are as tender as you like and the grill marks are showing. Season and serve.

Grill sweet potato planks (about ¼ to ½ inch thick, peeled or not, and brushed on both sides with oil), flipping to lightly caramelize each side. When softened, top with a thick sweep of apple butter and crunchy pecan pieces.

WAYS TO DRESS UP GRILLED VEGGIES

- **Top grilled vegetables** with melted browned butter or flavored nut oils just before serving.

- **Dip grilled veggie planks** in breadcrumbs and fry in butter and oil on both sides until crisp. Serve with a well-seasoned tomatoey dipping sauce, if you like.

- **Pile lightly cooked salmon or tuna** on top of grilled veggie planks. Finish them with a spoonful of seeds, and maybe a light touch of mayo mixed with herbs.

- **Spread grilled veggie planks** with guacamole, and top with beans of your choice, a few leafy greens, and dollops of hummus or some crumbled feta cheese.

- **Grill unpeeled eggplant planks** (about ½ to ¾ inch thick and brushed on both sides with oil), flipping when the first side is charred to your liking. When the planks are just soft and gently charred, top with slices of cheese. Keep the planks on the grill but move to a cooler spot till the cheese melts. As you serve, ladle on some tomato sauce and scatter fresh or dried herbs over the top.

Improv Curry

Cooking Circle member Kyle cooked all the evening meals on a 25-day camping trip with more than 30 people, 20 of whom were high school students. He cooked these meals without recipes, in a van with its passenger seats removed. Where the seats had been, a framework held coolers with ice (no refrigerator), two camp cookstoves powered with propane, and a heavy-duty stove for boiling water.

Kyle discovered the wonder of curries on the road.

....

I would start the dish with butter and coconut oil. When they melted, I added aromatics, which always included ginger. Then I put in a ton of chopped vegetables—sweet potatoes, carrots, green beans, bell peppers. When they were softened, I stirred in curry paste and coconut milk and cooked everything until the sauce reduced a bit.

My best dish was a chickpea curry because the seasonings really worked. I started the usual way with butter and coconut oil, then added cinnamon sticks, smashed garlic cloves, minced fresh ginger, and bay leaves. When the aromatics had released their flavor, I stirred in turmeric, salt, the chickpeas, and coconut milk and let the mixture cook down by about a third.

Near the end, I mixed in chopped garlic scapes that we had harvested along the way from a friendly church's garden. I also made scape pesto from what I had left and set it out for individuals to add if they wanted.

Oh, and I served the curry over quinoa. Great meal!

COOKING FLAVORFUL VEGETABLES

- **The vegetables you find in your pantry** have the advantage of being ready any time. Consider beans for sauces (whole or puréed), as toppings, and as partners in bowls, salads, and soups. Canned tomatoes (whole, stewed, or diced) deepen the flavor of soups and other roasted vegetables, and they brighten kale and chard. And what *can't* you do with artichokes?

- **Use tomatoes**—whether fresh or canned in the off-season—often in cooking because they make dishes less bland and act as a good base for a wide range of spices. —EVONNE

- **Whenever you make a pasta sauce** for your evening meal, make twice as much as you need so you've got a start the next time you need tomato sauce. —DARYL

- **If you make too much cauliflower, broccoli, or cabbage,** blend it, add some broth and a touch of half-and-half, heat it, and season it. You'll turn out a pretty great soup. —CHRISTINA

- **If you've overbought a particular vegetable**—or the garden is going wild—cook the vegetable you have in abundance all at once, but barely season it. That cooked vegetable becomes immediately available to be added to a future dish. And its minimal seasoning won't conflict with the way you finally decide to use it. —ZAHRA

- **When you're overloaded with veggies,** chop up whatever you've got, put them in small ziplock freezer bags, and label them. Freeze the works and use them later in a stir-fry. Add garlic and onions when you're ready to go. If you want, toss in chopped or shredded chicken, pork, or beef, fresh or left over. —LORRE

Margaret shared these great tips:

- **Sometimes corn can stand in for potatoes** in a soup, since they are both carbs. This helps with using up little bits of food you've accumulated in the freezer.

- **Firm green veggies** can be swapped pretty readily in recipes: broccoli, cauliflower, asparagus, and even snow peas can stand in for each other.

FREEZE ANY LEMONS AND LIMES that are going south, and when you need them, pull them out and zest the frozen fruit over stir-fried veggies, salads, and shrimp for an extra zip. Don't thaw the citrus first. Stir-fried or steamed green beans mixed with a light touch of mayo (instead of oil or butter) and then topped with frozen lemon or lime zest are a delight. —LORRE

Daryl shared these wonderful ideas:

- **Mix chickpeas** with lime, mint, and a little feta cheese. You'll
- have a super easy-to-prepare meal with a lot of nutrition combined with exploding flavors. Eat them with a grain, toast, or rice.

- **Sprinkle little red beans** with hot pepper or chipotle powder, some oregano, and lime juice for a Mexican feel. Serve over rice, with sour cream or plain yogurt on the side.

- **If you're weary of eggplant as the summer winds down,** make a big batch of baba ghanoush, spoon it into pint-sized boxes, and tuck it away in the freezer till you need a quick appetizer and you're once again hungry for eggplant.

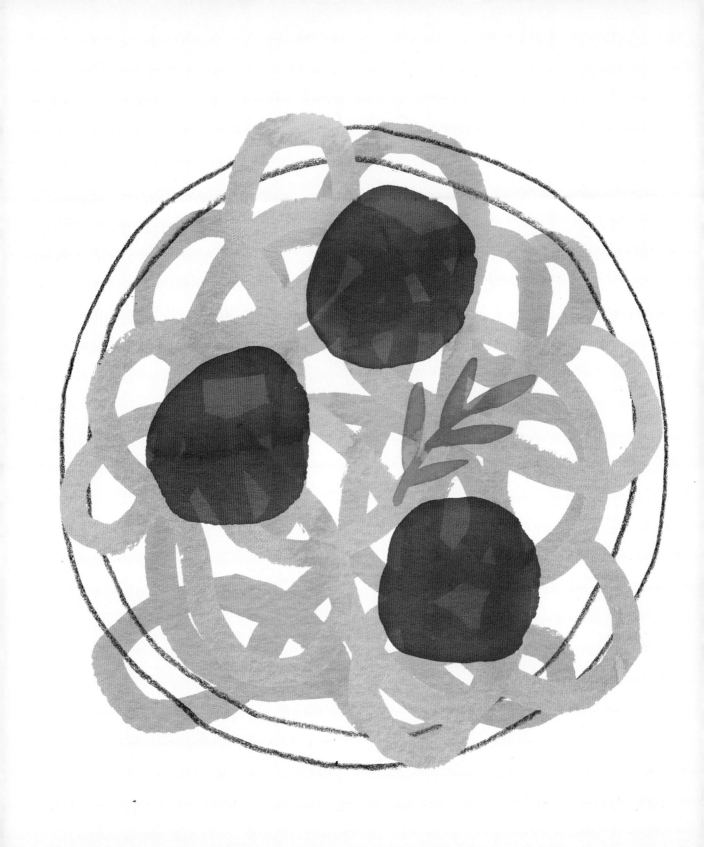

2 / PASTAS AND GRAINS

IN THE BALANCE BETWEEN TEXTURE AND FLAVOR, texture sneaks past flavor in importance when we're talking about pastas and grains. Get the cooking time right, as well as the amount of water and salt needed for cooking, and you'll have a good outcome.

Explore all the Italian pasta shapes, the varieties of Asian noodles, and all the available grains. It's helpful to keep notes about the cooking times and ratios of liquids to grains that you like best. But if you're not a note maker, follow the directions on the box. If you buy grains in bulk, purchase them from a store with a high turnover, such as a natural foods store. Check a trusted source on the internet, or the instructions for your electric pressure cooker, for how to cook the particular grain in the form you've bought.

When pairing your pasta or grain with a sauce, think open canvas:

- **Which toppings** work well with which bases?

- **How fancy** or how simple should the sauces be?

- **How thick** or slick?

- **What's a good overall balance** of pasta or grain to sauce?

COOKING PASTA

INGREDIENTS THAT WORK WELL

- **Quality pasta.** The best Italian and Italian-influenced pasta is made with durum wheat. The pasta's shape should hold the sauce that you plan to put over it.

- **Salt.** This is for the cooking water. Add plenty of it for the best flavor.

STEPS TO TAKE

1. **Put 5 quarts of water** in a 6-quart stockpot if you're making a pound of pasta. (For ½ pound of pasta, use 3 quarts of water.) Cover the pot and bring the water to a rolling boil.

2. **Stir a heaping tablespoon of salt** into the boiling water just before adding the pasta.

3. **Drop the pasta** into the boiling water, stirring as you go. This helps long strands of pasta relax into the water and circulates water through the pasta.

4. **Cook uncovered,** stirring now and then so that the pasta doesn't stick together. Maintain a boil while the pasta cooks. If you're in a hurry and decide to cover the pot, keep your eye on it because it can boil over easily.

5. **Plan ahead** to save some of the pasta cooking water. (You may need it to smooth out the sauce or unclump sticky pasta.) Set out a glass 2-cup measuring cup ahead of time, right next to the pot, so you don't automatically dump the water and forget this step. Just before draining the cooked pasta, you'll use the measuring cup to take a big scoop of the hot cooking water and set it aside.

6. **Use the directions on the package as a guide** for how long to cook the pasta. As it nears the end of its cooking time, fish out a piece and taste it. If it's almost done to your liking, save some cooking water, drain the pasta in a colander, then immediately put the pasta back in the pot to stay warm until serving time. It will continue to cook during these steps. If you've made the pasta for a salad, rinse it with cold water while it's in the colander so that it doesn't stick together, stirring to separate the pieces, if needed.

7. **Spoon on the sauce** (see Chapter 4 for ideas), adding just enough that every piece of pasta is coated but not drowning—assuming you want to experience the texture and flavor of the pasta itself. (If you're all about the sauce, heap it on!)

Instructions continue on page 66

WHEN YOU COOK, MAKE EXTRA "CORE INGREDIENTS," such as starches and proteins and sometimes vegetables, so you have them as leftovers for a future meal. This is important: *barely season them.* That way, you can mix and match those leftovers in later meals, going in whatever direction you feel like cooking that day.

Those leftover, lightly seasoned core ingredients are like a blank slate, allowing you now to introduce fresh vegetables, spices, herbs, and whatever else has caught your eye or made your mouth water. —ZAHRA

8. **If the sauce is thicker** than you want or it's hard to mix it through the pasta, stir in enough hot pasta cooking water to loosen it up.

Cooking Pasta in an Electric Pressure Cooker

Read your cooker's instructions for the type of pasta you're using to find out how much water to use and how long to cook it. Or cut in half the stovetop cooking time given on the pasta package, subtract 1 minute, and use high pressure. For example, if the pasta you're making needs 10 minutes of stovetop cooking time, divide 10 by 2 and subtract 1. Electric pressure cooking time = 4 minutes. Finish with a quick release.

Spoon the sauce over the pasta, making sure every piece is coated but not drowning in sauce.

Reserve some cooking water before draining the pasta in case you need to thin the sauce.

Pasta with Vegetables

IMAGINE YOU'RE MAKING A COLORFUL MOSAIC or a painting with food. Sauté the vegetables in olive oil, then arrange them in a spontaneous, vigorous way on top of the pasta. Black olives, shaved strips of squash, red and yellow grape or cherry tomatoes, grilled eggplant, snow peas, fresh basil leaves—you get the picture. —EUGENE

- **Cut up fresh tomatoes.** (Plum tomatoes are meatier than others. If you have an extra moment, peel the tomatoes and squeeze out the seeds to eliminate any hint of bitterness.) Add fresh herbs and seasonings. Or stir in grated cheese, red pepper flakes, sliced black olives, and/or capers.

- **Add chopped garlic and/or onions,** and maybe a chopped bell pepper, as a flavor enhancer to fresh, raw vegetables in a lemon butter sauce. Keep the sauce chunky or purée it.

- **Steam, sauté, roast, or microwave fresh cut-up vegetables**—asparagus, broccoli, carrots, sugar snap peas, red onions, bell peppers, summer squash. Add them, along with their pan drippings or cooking water, to the cooked and drained pasta.

- **Cook vegetables with the pasta** by tossing chopped, raw vegetables straight into the pot of pasta during its last several minutes of cooking time. Add denser vegetables (broccoli florets and stems, sliced leeks) about 3 minutes before the end of the cooking time; add less-dense and more delicate vegetables (chunked tomatoes, chopped zucchini) 1 to 2 minutes before the pasta is finished.

- **Make cauliflower Alfredo sauce,** as Christina does, by steaming a whole head of cauliflower, then puréeing it with milk and Parmesan cheese. Mix the sauce with the cooked pasta, crack an egg into it and mix again, then top it with shrimp. The sauce is a yummy binding agent.

- **Make creamy corn sauce** by lightly sautéing corn kernels (fresh, frozen, or canned) in butter. Stir in some pasta cooking water to make a saucy mixture. Buzz with your immersion blender to coarsely chop the corn and blend it with the cooking water. Season before stirring it into the cooked pasta.

- **Combine white wine and/or lemon juice,** olive oil or melted butter, sliced mushrooms (sautéed or raw), minced garlic, and seasonings and toss with the cooked pasta.

- **Toss the pasta with olive oil, grated cheese, and fresh herbs.** Or start with pesto and then decide whether and how much oil, cheese, and herbs to add. Surround with sautéed vegetables, grilled chicken, or whatever you have on hand. Include a few handfuls of chopped nuts, if you like.

- **Stir peas or chopped fresh spinach** into freshly cooked pasta. (The residual heat from the pasta will steam the fresh or frozen vegetables.) Or add chickpeas and season to taste.

Cut up a whole head of broccoli or cauliflower, or use half of each. Steam, sauté, roast, or microwave till quite soft. Mash. Mix into the cooked and drained pasta. Splash with olive oil or melted butter, herbs, and seasonings.

MAXIMIZING PASTA

- **Toss cooked pasta** into a pot with a little broth or reserved pasta cooking water—just enough to start to loosen it up. Stir in some melted butter and a little olive oil, then sprinkle it with Parmesan cheese and crack an egg on top. Stir it over low heat to get a delicious, creamy sauce that's perfect topped with grilled chicken and sautéed vegetables. — LINDSEY

- **Consider rice noodles** when you're camping. You won't be waiting a long time for water to boil or for a grain to cook to the perfect texture. Or start a pho early in the day in your slow cooker. Add rice noodles right at the end . . . 7 minutes and they're done! — KYLE

- **Try some less-common pastas** such as big rigatoni. Stuff strips of cheese into the uncooked noodles, then cover them with lots of tomato sauce so the noodles have enough liquid to soften while baking. Serve with a simple crushed-tomato sauce. Stuffed big shells are also a good alternative to lasagna. Stuff the uncooked shells with ricotta cheese, egg, and chopped parsley. Cover them with tomato sauce and bake. — EUGENE

- **Drop uncooked pasta** into simmering soup broth to give body to the soup and flavor to the pasta.

- **If you have leftover cooked, plain pasta,** use it as a base for a bowl.

- **Fold zesty dressing** into cooked pasta to loosen it up. Then gently stir in cooked and/or raw vegetables, cooked meat, and cheese for a pasta salad.

- **Mixing just two or three ingredients into your pasta** lets you taste and experience the texture of each one. On the other hand, more ingredients may add more interest. Go with your instincts—and what's in your pantry and fridge, and the amount of time you have.

- **Top any veggie-, seafood-, or meat-sauced pasta** with a green, lightly dressed salad. Serve immediately. The greens will wilt a little, but they're a bridge between crispy cool and warm.

- **Go broad with cheese.** Don't get stuck on Parmesan only. Crumble feta; break burrata; thinly slice Manchego, fontina, and/or Gouda; split up some Camembert. Mix it into the cooked pasta and sauce, or scatter it over the top.

Mix together melted butter, breadcrumbs (fresh or dried), a scant spoonful of horseradish or mustard, and a pinch of thyme. Spoon over the top of the pasta dish for an alternative to grated cheese. Broil briefly to brown the crumbs. You've just upped the flavor and the texture.

**Smoked salmon
or trout,** added
just before serving,
pairs beautifully
with fresh chives
and tomato sauce
on pasta.

Pasta with Meat or Seafood

KEEP SEVERAL CANS OF CHOPPED CLAMS ON HAND. They're your backup for making linguine with white clam sauce if you have drop-in guests. Invite your guests to help; it takes some heat off you, and you're all together while it's happening.

Clam sauce is really easy. Melt butter, add olive oil, then put in the clams along with their juice. The mixture usually needs very little salt. Heat the sauce gently; you don't want to cook the clams. Serve the linguine on a big family-style platter, pour on the sauce, and scatter a little chopped parsley over the top if you have it. Bread and salad finish the meal.

—EUGENE

- **Add chopped cooked bacon** or ham to a cream sauce.

- **Add cooked clams,** shrimp, chunked whitefish, or tuna to either a tomato-based sauce or an olive oil and white wine sauce. To prevent overcooking, add the seafood just before serving. Or add it raw and cook it gently in the sauce for only a few minutes.

- **Lightly brown ground beef and/or ground pork,** then add vegetables and seasonings, tomato sauce, beef stock, and red or white wine. Cook it long and slow so the liquid reduces. Stir often. Taste often. Add milk or cream near the end for a Bolognese finish.

- **Make meatballs** from ground beef and/or pork. Cook in the oven on a sheet pan, or on the stovetop in a skillet, until browned. Then add to a tomato sauce. You can substitute browned cut-up sausage for the meatballs.

- **Use leftover beef Burgundy,** as Jay does, to make a rich pasta sauce, along with every veg you find in the fridge!

Taste a few cooked grains (here, quinoa) near the end of the cooking time to check for doneness.

COOKING GRAINS

There is no single right way to cook grains. I hope you find that comforting and not alarming. Below are ways that I and the Cooking Circle members have found work for us. On your first time cooking any of these grains, think adventure.

INGREDIENTS THAT WORK WELL

- **barley** (hulled)
- **buckwheat**
- **bulgur**
- **cornmeal**
- **farro**
- **freekeh** (usually wheat; cracked)
- **Kamut**
- **millet** (hulled)
- **oats** (steel-cut)
- **quinoa**
- **rice** (white, brown, basmati, wild; long- or short-grain)
- **spelt**
- **teff**
- **wheat berries**

HINT

- **You're usually most successful** if you cook grains by themselves. But if different grains call for about the same amount of water and cooking time, you can easily cook them together to add more interest to your dish.

STEPS TO TAKE

The instructions below are for cooking grains on the stovetop. You can also cook grains in an electric pressure cooker, following the manufacturer's directions and the guidelines on page 77.

1. **Add the liquid** (usually water, although broth and stock are also good) and a heaping tablespoon of salt to a stockpot. Bring it to a boil. See the tables on pages 76 and 77 for the amount of liquid to use.

2. **Stir in** the grain. Grains don't need much babysitting.

3. **Boil gently, uncovered,** stirring occasionally. (Rice is the exception here. Cover it while it cooks and don't stir it.) Cook for the amount of time indicated in the cooking tables.

4. **Taste a few grains** near the end of the cooking time. If they're cooked as you like them, take the pot off the heat. Let stand for a few minutes, then drain any liquid that wasn't absorbed.

RICE IS A GREAT BASE for all kinds of experimentation. Stir in or top it with cooked meat, beans, mixed vegetables, tomatoes, and corn, with whatever seasonings are tempting you—and have a global experience. —JAY

Cooking Grains on the Stovetop

GRAIN (1 CUP)	LIQUID	COOKING TIME	FINISHED AMOUNT
Barley (hulled)	3 cups	45–60 minutes	3½ cups
Buckwheat	2 cups	20 minutes	4 cups
Bulgur	2 cups	10–12 minutes	3 cups
Cornmeal	4 cups	25–30 minutes	2½ cups polenta
Farro	2½ cups	25–40 minutes	3 cups
Freekeh (usually wheat; cracked)	2–2½ cups	20–25 minutes	3 cups
Kamut	4 cups	Soak 8 hours; cook 45–60 minutes	3 cups
Millet (hulled)	2½ cups	20 minutes	4 cups
Oats (steel-cut)	4 cups	20 minutes	4 cups
Quinoa	2 cups	12–15 minutes	3¼ cups
Rice, brown	2½ cups	45 minutes	3–4 cups
Rice, white, long-grain	2 cups	25 minutes	4 cups
Rice, wild	3 cups	45–55 minutes	3½ cups
Spelt	4 cups	Soak 8 hours; cook 45–60 minutes	3 cups
Teff	3 cups	15–20 minutes	3 cups
Wheat berries	4 cups	Soak 8 hours; cook 45–60 minutes	3 cups

Adapted from Oldways Whole Grains Council, www.wholegrainscouncil.org

KITCHEN CHEAT SHEET
Cooking Grains in an Electric Pressure Cooker

GRAIN (1 CUP)	LIQUID	COOKER TIME	OPENING METHOD
Barley (hulled)	2 cups	20 minutes, high	10 minutes, natural
Buckwheat	2 cups	3 minutes, high	10 minutes, natural
Bulgur	3 cups	10 minutes, high	10 minutes, natural
Cornmeal	4 cups	25 minutes, high	Natural
Farro	2½ cups	10 minutes, high	Natural
Freekeh (usually wheat; cracked)	1⅔ cups	10 minutes, high	Natural
Kamut	2 cups	Soak 8 hours; cook 18 minutes, high	Natural
Millet (hulled)	1½ cups	1 minute, high	10 minutes, natural
Oats (steel-cut)	3 cups	10 minutes, high	Natural
Quinoa	1½ cups	1 minute, high	Natural
Rice, brown	1¼ cups	25 minutes, high	Natural
Rice, white, long-grain	1¼–1½ cups	5 minutes, high	Natural
Rice, wild	3 cups	25 minutes, high	Natural
Spelt	2½ cups	Soak 8 hours; cook 10 minutes, high	Natural
Teff	2 cups	2–3 minutes, high	Quick
Wheat berries	3 cups	Soak 8 hours; cook 40 minutes, high	Natural

77

Cook wild rice and brown rice together, in equal proportion in the same pot. The flavor of the wild rice shines, while you get bulk from the brown. It turns out to be a less expensive dish without sacrificing flavor. To make it sing after it's fully cooked, stir in sliced mushrooms, chopped walnuts, edamame, and dried cranberries. —DARYL

Cooked Grains and Company

Substitute these cooked grains for each other freely, wildly, madly. Seriously. Or mix them. What follows are just suggestions to poke your imagination.

- **Top polenta** with crumbled browned sausage and creamy corn.

- **Add leftover rice to a stir-fry.** Leftover rice is ideal here; the textures all work better if the rice is cooked and cold. Stir-fry thinly sliced meat till just cooked. Lift it out of the hot skillet and set it aside while you stir-fry cubed or sliced fresh vegetables. Fold in the already-cooked rice. When it's warmed, stir the meat back in. Season to taste. Break an egg or two into the hot food and stir quickly to bring everything together.

- **Mix together finely chopped cabbage,** cilantro, and scallions with hoisin sauce—all the ingredients that would flavor spring rolls—as Margaret does. Then pile the mix on top of hot rice (or hot rice noodles) and sprinkle everything with chopped peanuts. It's a balanced meal with a contrast in textures and flavors that people love!

- **Mix citrus into quinoa**, as Kyle likes to do. Use clementines, and then add apples, raisins, balsamic vinaigrette, massaged kale, onions, and/or arugula.

- **Before cooking quinoa,** sauté it in olive oil and add fresh garlic and other herbs you have on hand, such as fresh basil, the way that Lorre does. Consider using chicken broth as the liquid. When the quinoa is cooked and cooled, toss in fresh asparagus tips and roasted red peppers. Mushrooms, too, if you have them. If you're serving the dish alongside fish, grate lemon zest over the top.

- **Cook quinoa and grits together,** as Chuck suggests. The preferred formula is ¾ cup quinoa to 1 cup grits. For the first meal, serve them soft and hot, topped with steak and a Provençal sauce. Then fully chill the leftover cooked grains in a loaf pan. When they've set up, cut them into slices and fry them in a bit of oil. Serve those crispy slices with eggs, sausage, and maple syrup, or as the crispy carbohydrate in a Thai salad, or as a polenta-type element for an Italian dish.

Pairings continue on page 80

GRAIN AND PASTA DISHES ARE GREAT FOR A POTLUCK OR CARRY-IN. You can serve them warm, at room temperature, or cold. A rice-based dish with beans, tomatoes, salsa, cilantro, and Mexican seasoning is good at any temperature. Or mix the rice, beans, and tomatoes with Italian flavors instead—try fresh basil and oregano, and an oil and vinegar dressing in place of salsa. —EVONNE

IF YOU'RE NOT CRAZY ABOUT BROWN RICE
but want to offset the fact that white rice converts rather quickly into sugar in the human body, use this clever hack that my Dominican friend taught me: cook white rice and bulgur together, 1 part bulgur with 4 parts rice. Bulgur is a whole-grain cracked wheat that has been parboiled before being packaged. It cooks in the same time and with roughly the same amount of liquid as white rice. It does little to change the flavor of the rice, but it adds whole-grain fiber to the white rice, which has been polished free of its own fiber.

—DARYL

- **Top grains with roasted Brussels sprouts** and fresh avocado slices, drizzled with maple syrup and balsamic vinegar.

- **Spoon sautéed broccoli,** chopped raw spinach, chopped peanuts, and your favorite Asian sauce over the grains.

- **Try stir-fried green beans and scrambled eggs,** cooked lightly with sliced scallions, and a dash of walnut oil on top of or mixed into the grains.

- **Choose a variety of your favorite mushrooms.** Slice or quarter them. Sauté some and leave the rest raw. Stir into the cooked grain, along with the mushrooms' cooking liquid. Season to taste.

- **Spoon a thick layer of Greek yogurt** over the bottom of a good-sized platter. Season with salt, freshly ground black pepper, and chopped onions or garlic. Mix cooked barley or wheat berries together with whatever seeds you're hungry for, along with some oil and lemon juice. Fold in leafy greens, some herbs, and a cubed vegetable (cooked or raw). Spoon over the seasoned spread of yogurt.

- **Cook some bulgur or millet.** Meanwhile, mix together chickpeas, sliced fresh spinach, chopped red onion, and fresh or dried thyme. Decide whether or not to cook the chickpea mixture in butter and oil or keep it raw. Fold into the cooked grains or spoon the vegetables (and their sauce, if you've cooked them) over the top. Squeeze fresh lemon juice over everything.

- **Stir cooked farro,** cooked and diced bacon, lemon zest, grated Parmesan or a sharp cheddar, and toasted hazelnuts together. Add sautéed chopped broccoli or cauliflower if you're in the mood for vegetables, too. Eat the dish warm or cold.

- **Make grain-based turkey stuffing,** like Gini does. It involves both wild and long-grain white rice, dried apricots, orange juice, and more traditional stuffing items like roughly chopped onions and celery. Gini's mom cooks it pilaf-style. A mix of chicken stock and orange juice is the base liquid. She softens the onions and celery with butter in a saucepan before mixing in the uncooked rice, apricots, and liquid. Then the whole works goes into a casserole dish and on into the oven. She finishes it with toasted pine nuts and chopped parsley after she pulls it out of the oven.

- **Brown steel-cut oats** in a bit of butter before cooking them. Cut unpeeled apples over the cooked oats and add fresh or frozen blueberries,

LENTILS COOK
IN THE SAME
AMOUNT OF TIME

as brown rice, so make
a pilaf by mixing those
two. —MARGARET

grated coconut, chopped nuts, and lots of plain yogurt. Drizzle maple syrup over everything if you're low on fruit. This is bliss for a texture nut, and it's wonderfully flavorful.

- **Combine uncooked buckwheat** with uncooked oats and wheat germ, coconut, cashews, unsweetened cocoa powder, brown sugar, sesame seeds, honey, and oil on a sheet pan. Bake at 325°F (170°C) for 10 to 15 minutes, or until brown and crunchy.

- **Use a variety of grains** to make pancakes the way that Daryl suggests. You can start with a base of rolled oats. (Please, there is no need to use quick oats! Just let the pancake batter rest a minute or two after you add the liquid so the oats can absorb it.) Then throw in whatever flours you have—buckwheat, cornmeal, rye, even teff flour. A minute or less is all that's needed to allow the grains to blend into the rest of the batter.

GRAIN-COOKING TIPS

- **Speed up the cooking time** by soaking the uncooked grains for several hours in the amount of liquid called for.

- **If the grains stick to the bottom of the pot** while cooking, take the pot off the heat, stir in ¼ cup or so of liquid, cover the pot, and let it stand for 5 to 10 minutes. That should loosen the stuck grains.

- **Cook double the amount of grains** you're making for your immediate needs so you have a good start on your next meal. Package up what you don't need immediately in meal-sized portions. Store them in the fridge or freezer for upcoming meals. If you want to warm the grains, stir in a little water or broth and heat them gently (microwaves do this well), stirring now and then to keep them from clumping together or sticking to the bottom of the pot.

- **If you don't have the time to cook grains from scratch,** pick up precooked grains at the store. Find them in the grains and/or freezer aisles. They're good, too, and they work.

3 / BIG PROTEINS

HERE'S A GOOD GUIDE to preparing some popular big proteins (chicken, turkey, pork, beef, and fish), the ideal cooking methods for each, and approximately how long it takes to cook various cuts. You're halfway to a good dish when you've discovered these basics.

You can approach this chapter in either of two ways: Start with the meat you have and choose the cooking method that best suits it. Or think first about how much time you have, then choose the meat that will cook well in that amount of time. While the meat cooks—if it doesn't need a lot of your attention—prep whatever you want to eat with it.

If you have more meat than you can eat in one meal, consider cooking it all at once and then cutting, shredding, or crumbling it up and storing it in the fridge or freezer in meal-sized portions. Do that, and you'll have made a big deposit into your meal-prep bank. You can eventually mix that meaty gold into salads or creamy sauces, scatter it over bowls, or use it to flavor soups. Guaranteed, you'll think of more ways to enjoy it.

Meat Cooking Techniques and Times by Cut

MEAT CUT	SIZE	COOKING TECHNIQUE	COOKING TIME
Chicken			
Breasts (boneless, skinless)	½" thick	Sauté (page 90) or broil (page 95)	Sauté 4–6 minutes or broil 5–10 minutes or until meat is at recommended temperature (page 87)
Cutlets	½" thick	Sauté (page 90) or broil (page 95)	Sauté 4–6 minutes or broil 5–10 minutes or until meat is at recommended temperature (page 87)
Legs and thighs (boneless)	4–6 ounces each	Sear (page 97)	15–20 minutes or until meat is at recommended temperature (page 87)
Legs and thighs (bone-in)	6–8 ounces each	Roast (page 104)	40–55 minutes or until meat is at recommended temperature (page 87)
Whole chicken	3–6 pounds	Roast (page 101)	15–20 minutes per pound or until meat is at recommended temperature (page 87)
Turkey			
Cutlets	½" thick	Sauté (page 90) or broil (page 95)	Sauté 4–6 minutes or broil 5–10 minutes or until meat is at recommended temperature (page 87)
Legs, thighs, or breasts (bone-in or boneless)	6–8 ounces each	Roast (page 106)	15–20 minutes per pound or until meat is at recommended temperature (page 87)

MEAT CUT	SIZE	COOKING TECHNIQUE	COOKING TIME
Pork			
Boneless chops	1" thick	Sauté (page 90) or broil (page 95)	Sauté 4–6 minutes or broil 5–10 minutes or until meat is at recommended temperature (page 87)
Butt (a.k.a. Boston butt)	3–4 pounds	Roast (page 111) or stew (page 117)	1 hour 30 minutes to 1 hour 45 minutes or until meat is at recommended temperature (page 87)
Fresh ham	2–3 pounds	Roast (page 111)	1 hour 30 minutes to 1 hour 45 minutes or until meat is at recommended temperature (page 87)
Loin roast with bone	3–4 pounds	Roast (page 111)	1 hour 30 minutes to 1 hour 45 minutes or until meat is at recommended temperature (page 87)
Medallions	1" thick	Sauté (page 90) or broil (page 95)	Sauté 4–6 minutes or broil 5–10 minutes or until meat is at recommended temperature (page 87)
Picnic ham	4–5 pounds	Braise (page 115)	2–3 hours in the oven or until meat is at recommended temperature (page 87)
Shoulder	3–4 pounds	Roast (page 111) or stew (page 117)	1 hour 30 minutes to 1 hour 45 minutes or until meat is at recommended temperature (page 87)
Spareribs	3 pounds, cut into serving-size pieces	Roast (page 111)	1 hour 30 minutes to 1 hour 45 minutes or until meat is at recommended temperature (page 87)

Chart continues on page 86

Meat Cooking Techniques and Times by Cut (continued)

MEAT CUT	SIZE	COOKING TECHNIQUE	COOKING TIME
Beef			
Boneless rib-eye roast	3–4 pounds	Roast (page 109)	20–25 minutes per pound or until meat is at recommended temperature (page 87)
Brisket	3–4 pounds	Braise (page 115) or stew (page 117)	2–3 hours in the oven or until meat is at recommended temperature (page 87)
Burgers	6–8 ounces each	Sear (page 97)	4–6 minutes or until meat is at recommended temperature (page 87)
Chuck roast (a.k.a. arm or English roast)	3–4 pounds	Roast (page 109) or stew (page 117)	20–25 minutes per pound or until meat is at recommended temperature (page 87)
Short ribs	3–4 pounds	Roast (page 109) or braise (page 115)	20–25 minutes per pound or until meat is at recommended temperature (page 87)
Steak	1"–1¼" thick	Sear (page 97)	4–6 minutes or until meat is at recommended temperature (page 87)
Strip roast	3–4 pounds	Roast (page 109)	20–25 minutes per pound or until meat is at recommended temperature (page 87)
Tenderloin roast	3–4 pounds	Roast (page 109)	20–25 minutes per pound or until meat is at recommended temperature (page 87)
Top round roast	3–4 pounds	Roast (page 109) or stew (page 117)	20–25 minutes per pound or until meat is at recommended temperature (page 87)
Fish			
Fillets	½"–1" thick	Sauté (page 90) or broil (page 95)	Sauté 4–6 minutes or broil 5–10 minutes or until fish is at recommended temperature (page 87)
Sturdy fish, such as salmon, tuna, swordfish, monkfish, or shark	1"–1¼" thick	Sear (page 97)	4–6 minutes or until fish is at recommended temperature (page 87)

Meat Cooking Temperatures

Because it's nearly impossible to rescue overcooked meat, and because I think that the flavor and texture of many cuts of meat are compromised by overcooking them, I lean toward cooking to a lower temperature than USDA recommendations. I've listed both temperatures so that you can decide for yourself which you prefer.

MEAT	MY PREFERRED TEMP	USDA TEMP
Beef (rare)	115°F–120°F (46°C–49°C)	*
Beef (medium rare)	120°F–125°F (49°C–52°C)	*
Beef (medium)	125°F–135°F (52°C–57°C)	*
Beef (medium well)	135°F–150°F (57°C–66°C)	*
Beef (well)	145°F–160°F (63°C–71°C)	145°F (63°C)
Chicken	150°F (66°C)	165°F (74°C)
Fish	140°F (60°C)	145°F (63°C)
Pork	140°F (60°C)	145°F (63°C)
Turkey	150°F (66°C)	165°F (74°C)

*Note: The USDA recommends cooking all beef to an internal temperature of at least 145°F (63°C).

Ground Meat Three Ways

FOR A LOW-CARB, SHELL-LESS TACO PIE, brown some ground beef; stir in ground cumin, chili powder, a little salsa, and a couple of eggs; top the mixture with cheese; and bake.

When it comes time to serve, put out a spread of options for toppings and let everyone add what they like: diced fresh tomatoes, sour cream, diced avocado or guacamole, red onion and/or scallions, pickled jalapeños, fresh cilantro. This one is a crowd-pleaser!

—LINDSEY

One day my husband comes in from the store with a gigantic package of ground turkey. We like turkey meatloaf, but this amount was clearly going to make several meals, and I didn't want to freeze the meat before cooking it.

My first thought was meatloaf, meatballs, and stuffed bell peppers. They all use the same meat base and nearly the same other ingredients. So I combined everything I wanted to mix together—the meat, salsa (so I wouldn't have to chop all the bell peppers and onions), breadcrumbs, salt, black pepper, and eggs. Then I divided the mixture into thirds and made the three different dishes.

I baked all three at the same temperature and time (350°F/180°C for about an hour). We ate the stuffed peppers for dinner; I popped the meatloaf and meatballs into the freezer.

When I have to put a meal on the table fast, I can pull out an already prepped and cooked dish from the freezer. It means some preplanning and weekend cooking, but it beats a panicked midweek.

What Can You Do with Ground Meat?

- **Brown** it on the stovetop and top it with a sauce. Ground meat is quick to brown if you're short on time. Or prep the meat ahead and freeze it for another time.
- **Bake** it in the oven.
- **Broil** it.
- **Grill** it.
- **Crumble** it, cooked or uncooked, into a mixture of vegetables or soup broth.

TIPS FROM THE COOKING CIRCLE
COOKING BIG PROTEINS

- **Pork, chicken, tofu, and tempeh** are fairly interchangeable when it comes to cooking methods. — GINI

- **If you're cooking on the stovetop,** bring your meat to room temperature before you begin cooking. It will respond more quickly to the hot skillet than if it came straight out of the fridge.

- **Use a skillet** that will accommodate all the meat you're preparing—but *don't crowd the pieces.* Leave a little space between them (or about 1 inch if you're searing them), or else they'll steam in each other's juices rather than brown. If you don't have a big enough skillet, cook the meat in batches.

SAUTÉING

Advantages: Sautéing is quick and easy and gives a light finish to the meat. It also produces delicious drippings, which you can drizzle over the finished meat or use as the base for making a quick, flavorful sauce.

STEPS TO TAKE

1. **Put a mixture** of oil and butter into an unheated skillet. (Butter brings the flavor; oil keeps it from burning because it has a higher smoking point than butter.)

2. **Heat the skillet** over medium heat. When you're ready to add the meat to the skillet, increase the heat to medium-high.

3. **Carefully place the meat** in the skillet, laying one end of the meat into the part of the skillet closest to you, and slowly lowering the rest of the piece away from you. That reduces the chance you'll be splattered with oil.

4. **Sauté** for 2 to 3 minutes, or until the meat is lightly browned.

5. **Flip it over** and sauté for 2 to 3 minutes longer, again just until the meat is lightly browned.

6. **Remove the meat** from the heat when the interior registers the temperature noted on page 87. (This temperature allows for the fact that the meat will continue to cook even after you remove it from the heat and it's resting.)

7. **Immediately put the meat** on plates or a platter. Tent it with foil to keep it warm.

HINTS

- **Chicken breasts (boneless, skinless)** and chicken and turkey cutlets should be ½ inch thick.
- **Pork medallions** and boneless chops should be 1 inch thick.
- **Fish fillets** thinner than 1 inch thick should be doubled over.

MAKE YOUR OWN HERB- OR CITRUS- FLAVORED BUTTER and lay a chunk on each individual serving. Here's a formula to start with: Mix together 8 tablespoons (1 stick) of softened butter, 1 teaspoon of fresh lemon juice, and 2 tablespoons of one or several chopped fresh herbs (sage, marjoram, thyme, rosemary, oregano, basil, parsley, chives, dill). Taste. Add salt and freshly ground black pepper or any other seasonings you want. Refrigerate until firm, then slice and serve.

FINISHING

1. **Use wine** to make a sauce from the drippings (see page 92), if you like.

2. **Taste the sauce.** If it's too sharp, add some broth to round off the flavor, and/or a tablespoon or so of butter or cream to mellow it.

3. **If you want to add extras** to the sauce, now's the time. Stir in mustard or capers; dried or fresh herbs; dried or fresh fruit; anchovies or black olives; chopped tomatoes, onions, and/or mushrooms; and/or chutney or horseradish. Taste the sauce to make sure you like its seasonings. Then spoon it over the meat.

FREESTYLE SAUCE FROM DRIPPINGS

Here's how to deglaze your skillet to make a rich and savory sauce.

How to Wing It

Heat the skillet so the drippings are warm and loose.

Deglaze the skillet by pouring in a glug of wine or any of the other acids listed in the column to the left. Using a wooden spoon, firmly stir loose any browned bits that are sticking to the skillet. Blend them into the drippings.

Stir in the stock. Bring the mixture to a boil.

Cook over medium heat, stirring occasionally, until the sauce becomes syrupy.

Season to taste with salt and pepper, then add whatever other seasonings the developing sauce might need.

Remove from the heat when you're happy with the flavor and consistency. If you'd like the sauce to be creamier or less sharp, stir in some milk. Add butter, too, if you want a glossy finish.

INGREDIENTS THAT WORK WELL

- **drippings** from having sautéed or seared meat, vegetables, tofu, or tempeh in your skillet
- **an acid** (wine, vinegar, or lemon, lime, or tomato juice)
- **stock or broth**
- **salt and freshly ground black pepper**
- **seasonings**
- **whole milk or cream**
- **butter**

Punch to Drippings

- **Onion-mushroom sauce:** After deglazing the skillet, stir in sliced onions, shallots, or scallions, along with sliced mushrooms, letting them sauté in the drippings until they're as soft as you like. Then stir in the stock, cook, and season to taste.

- **Mustardy sauce:** Add some mustard when you add the butter. This is especially good with chicken and fish.

- **Curry sauce:** Add curry powder, honey, and mustard when you add the butter, as Beth does. Drip the final sauce over pork chops or chicken.

- **Lemon-herb sauce:** Add fresh herbs after you add the stock, along with the juice of half a lemon. Add half a head of garlic, minced, too, if that sounds good.

- **Deeper, darker sauce for beef:** Add ketchup and Worcestershire sauce once you remove the sauce from the heat.

- **Red wine reduction sauce:** Sauté fresh garlic and sliced mushrooms in a mixture of half olive oil, half butter, the way that Lorre does. Add half a bottle of red wine. Stir everything together, then let it reduce by half over medium-low heat. Reduce the heat and stir in 4 tablespoons of butter cut into chunks. You could also add a tablespoon or so of jam . . . fig preserves are Lorre's favorite. Try pouring this over a pork tenderloin with some rosemary while it's roasting!

Meat should be ½ to 1 inch thick for best results.

BROILING

Advantages: Broiling quickly adds a browned finish to both sides of the meat. It deepens the flavor, too, while retaining the meat's juices.

HINTS

- **Begin by placing your food 4 to 5 inches below the heat source** in the oven. Raise or lower the oven rack as needed.
- **Meat should be ½ to 1 inch thick,** but be sure to keep your eye on it while it broils. If you broil a thicker cut of meat, it's possible to burn the outside before the inside is cooked enough.

STEPS TO TAKE

1. **Preheat the broiler** for about 5 minutes.

2. **Lay the meat** on a baking sheet or in a sturdy cast-iron skillet that's broiler safe.

3. **Cook one side** for about two-thirds of the total cooking time. Most foods broil fully in 5 to 10 minutes. For example, if you think the food will be fully cooked the way you want it in 5 minutes, broil the first side for just a bit over 3 minutes.

4. **Use an instant-read meat thermometer** to check how close the food is to the ultimate temperature you're aiming for, then flip it over to continue broiling for about 2 minutes, or more or less, depending on what the thermometer told you.

5. **Remove the meat** from the heat source when the interior registers the temperature noted on page 87. (This temperature allows for the fact that the meat will continue to cook even after you remove it from the heat and it's resting.)

6. **If you want the broiled meat to cook a little more,** but you don't want to risk burning it, move the meat to a lower oven rack so it's at least 10 inches below the broiler yet benefiting from its indirect heat, or microwave it for a minute or so.

The meat is ready to flip when the crust is brown and you can easily lift the whole piece off the pan.

SEARING

Advantages: The direct contact the meat has with a fire-hot skillet puts an immediate browned finish on it. It happens fast, and you are right there to watch for and smell when it's done the job—but before it's gone too far.

HINTS

- **Do *not* use a nonstick skillet** for searing. It won't allow a crusty finish to form.
- **Eighty percent lean ground chuck is delicious;** there is no need to rub burgers made from it with oil before searing them.
- **Steak and sturdy fish** should be 1 to 1¼ inches thick.

STEPS TO TAKE

1. **Heat the skillet slowly** over low heat for about 10 minutes until it's hot through. That will ensure that its temperature won't drop far when you put the meat in.

2. **Increase the heat** to high. Let the empty skillet heat for a few minutes longer.

3. **Prepare the meat** while you wait. Pat the meat dry, then rub both sides of the meat generously with oil. (Skip this step if you're making burgers from 80% lean ground beef.) Season it on all sides with plenty of salt and freshly ground black pepper.

4. **Lay one end** of the meat into the part of the skillet closest to you, and slowly lower the rest of the piece away from you. This reduces the chances you'll be splattered with hot oil. Sear the meat for 2 to 3 minutes.

5. **Try to lift a corner** of the meat with a metal spatula. If the meat shows a brown crust on the bottom, and if you can lift the whole piece with very little resistance, it's ready to be flipped over so the other side can sear. If it sticks, let it sear a bit longer, but stay close and don't let it burn. Then flip.

6. **Check the meat** with an instant-read meat thermometer when the second side has formed a crust, to make sure it's cooked almost to the temperature you want (see page 87). If it is, remove the meat from the skillet immediately.

Instructions continue on page 98

7. **If you have a good sear** on both sides of the meat but want a more fully cooked interior, transfer the meat to a platter and tent it with foil to keep it warm. Add a short glug of wine, broth, or tomato, lemon, or lime juice to the hot skillet. Use a wooden spoon to stir loose any browned bits left in the skillet from searing the meat.

8. **Return the meat to the skillet** and sauce (see page 91). Cover the skillet and cook over medium heat until the interior of the meat reaches the temperature you want. Or place the covered skillet (make sure it's ovenproof) in a 350°F (180°C) oven and let it roast until just before it reaches the temperature you want.

I PREFER STEAKS IN THE SKILLET to the grill because I can retain so much more of the flavor and juices that would have disappeared into the fire. —CHUCK

If You're Tempted to Do This, *STOP*!

>> **Put cold meat into the skillet** and figure it will warm up. Well, it will, but it's unlikely to develop the crusty, browned finish that happens when a room-temperature piece of meat meets a sizzling-hot skillet. It's likely to burn on the outside before it's cooked on the inside.

INSTEAD: Get the meat out of the fridge 30 minutes before you're ready to begin cooking it. Unwrap it and let it sit on a platter or plate until it reaches room temperature.

>> **Put your meat in a cold skillet** and hope for a good sear.

INSTEAD: Heat your skillet as described above and rub all sides of the meat with oil *before* putting it in the skillet.

>> **Try to turn the meat over** before it has a good crusty finish on the first side, even when it doesn't want to let go of the skillet.

INSTEAD: Push at one corner of the meat with a metal spatula to see if you can gently budge it loose. And check to see if it's browned well. If it's a yes to both, the meat is ready to be turned. If it's a no to either, let it sear a little longer.

>> **Shove the meat around** in the skillet while it's searing.

INSTEAD: Leave it alone so it can build up a browned crust. If you keep it in motion, it won't be able to develop a crusty finish.

>> **Cook with too-low heat,** maybe because you're worried about burning the meat.

INSTEAD: Start by placing the empty skillet over low heat for about 10 minutes so it heats through, then jack up the heat to high for 2 to 3 minutes before laying the meat into the skillet. Now you're on your way to a sturdy sear.

If you roast poultry with the skin on, brush the skin with white vinegar, then sprinkle the bird liberally with salt. It gives the crunchy skin an extra dimension that is much like salt and vinegar chips. And it seeps into the meat underneath, giving it similar flavors that go so well with any potato accompaniment.

—ZAHRA

ROASTING A WHOLE CHICKEN

Advantages: Moderate oven heat cooks the meat slowly so that it doesn't dry out or burn. Over time it browns the surface, giving succulent flavor and a somewhat crispy finish. As you balance these two hoped-for outcomes, consider if and when to cover the roasting pan.

STEPS TO TAKE

1. **Take the chicken** out of the fridge 45 to 60 minutes before roasting it. If the butcher has wrapped the heart, liver, and gizzard in paper and put them in the cavity, remove them. (Cook them on the stovetop in water for a tasty broth and flavoring.)

2. **Pat** the chicken dry.

3. **Preheat the oven** to 425°F (220°C).

4. **Rub the chicken** all over with oil. Then season it generously with salt and pepper.

5. **Tie it up** with twine, if desired, and put it in the roasting container. If you want to add vegetables or sauce to the chicken, see pages 102–103.

6. **Roast** a 3-pound whole trussed chicken for 45 to 50 minutes. Stick an instant-read meat thermometer into the thick part of the thigh, but not against a bone. The chicken is done when the thermometer registers 150°F (66°C) to 165°F (74°C).

7. **Remove the chicken** from the oven and let it rest for 10 minutes. Then cut it into pieces and serve with the browned bits, if desired (see Save the Browned Bits!, page 103).

8. **Debone any leftovers** from the first meal. Hang on to the carcass (see page 208 for how to turn the bones into well-flavored bone broth). Store the meat in a tightly covered container in the fridge for a day or two. Turn this cubed, chunked, or shredded chicken into chicken salad. Add it to a green, grain, or vegetable salad. Build a bowl with it, stir it into soup, or make a broth-based sauce or gravy and mix it in.

IF YOU PLAN TO INCORPORATE THIS MEAT INTO SEVERAL MEALS, limit the amount of seasoning that you rub into whatever you're roasting. Adding heat such as cayenne or ground chiles is okay as long as you think all of the future dishes you'll make with this meat would be okay with it. Keeping the seasoning simple allows you to head in a variety of directions when you use the rest of the meat in upcoming meals.

—ZAHRA

Instructions continue on page 102

IF YOU WANT TO ADD VEGETABLES . . .

1. **Wash your vegetables,** such as white and sweet potatoes, red and yellow onions, leeks, carrots and parsnips, or green beans and broccoli.

2. **Cut the vegetables into chunks** that are slightly bigger than bite-size. Toss them with olive oil and your favorite seasonings.

3. **Settle the vegetables** next to the meat, ideally in a single layer. Or if the skillet or roasting pan is already full with the chicken, grease another baking pan and fork in the prepped vegetables, preferably in one layer so they all have direct contact with the pan surface and roast evenly.

When you bake chicken, consider adding celery, onion, carrot, some chopped bell pepper, and possibly canned peach slices and their juice. Use the broth to make a gravy or sauce for the finished chicken. If the fruit holds up in the baking, spoon it over or mix it into cooked rice alongside the chicken.

—BETH

IF YOU WANT TO SAUCE THE CHICKEN . . .

After the bird has roasted for 30 minutes or so:

- **Spoon barbecue sauce over it** and roast it for 10 to 20 minutes longer, or until the chicken is cooked through and the sauce has browned.

- **Drop chopped fresh mushrooms** over the browning bird, then pour 2 cups of hot cream over the top. Continue roasting for 10 to 20 minutes, or until the chicken is cooked through and the sauce is warm.

- **Make a sauce** from fresh lemon juice, olive oil, chopped garlic and onions, and fresh or dried thyme. Spoon over the roasting chicken. Continue roasting for 10 to 20 minutes, or until the chicken is cooked through and the sauce is warm.

- **Use the back of a spoon** to rub grainy mustard over the roasting bird. Mix fresh bread cubes or crumbs with melted butter and pat them onto the mustard-coated chicken. Continue roasting for 10 to 20 minutes, or until the chicken is cooked through and the bread is golden brown.

Save the Browned Bits!

Before you clean up the skillet, roasting pan, or sheet pan you used to roast your chicken, set it over medium heat on your stovetop (you might need to use two burners). Pour in a splash of white wine to help loosen the browned bits stuck to the surface. Stir with a little oomph to lift the bits. Cook until reduced slightly, then pour the syrupy sauce over the meat before serving it or storing it.

ROASTING BONE-IN CHICKEN LEGS AND THIGHS

Advantages: Same as for roasting a whole chicken (see page 101)

TRY PLAIN YOGURT as a go-to marinade and meat tenderizer. It not only tenderizes but adds a pleasant sourness much like that in sourdough bread. To the yogurt, add heaps of freshly grated ginger, a moderate amount of minced or sliced garlic, paprika, cumin, coriander, turmeric, salt, and then something sweet like tomato paste or palm sugar, which brings it all together in a mouthwatering way.

If you want perfection and the weather is cooperating, throw the meat on the grill, which adds smokiness and finger-licking goodness!

—ZAHRA

STEPS TO TAKE

1. **Take the chicken** out of the fridge 45 to 60 minutes before roasting it.

2. **Preheat the oven** to 425°F (220°C).

3. **Add butter and oil** (ideally in a 1:1 ratio) to an ovenproof skillet or roasting pan.

4. **Decide what kind of finish** you want on the roasted bird (see the three options—simply seasoned, oven-fried crust with breadcrumbs, and oven-fried crust with flour—that follow).

5. **Lay the prepped meat** in a single layer, skin-side down, in the fat in the skillet or roasting pan. Turn it over immediately to roast, skin-side up.

6. **Roast** for 30 to 35 minutes, or until the meat is loosening from the bone.

7. **Reduce the oven temperature** to 375°F (190°C). Flip each piece over. Spoon any of your favorite sauces over the chicken, or scatter dried herbs over the top.

8. **Return the meat** to the oven and roast for 10 to 20 minutes longer, until the sauce is hot and bubbly. Scatter fresh herbs over the top just before serving, if you like.

FOR A SIMPLY SEASONED FINISH

1. **Wiggle the skin loose** on the legs and thighs (but don't remove it).

2. **Spread salt and pepper** on the meat under the skin.

3. **Put the skin** back in place.

MAKE AN EXTRA-BIG HELPING of herbed chicken thighs. When they're fully cooked, deboned, and cubed, add some to groundnut stew, pasta, or kale salad. (I had some with a soft-boiled egg yesterday for breakfast!) —GINI

FOR AN OVEN-FRIED CRUST WITH BREADCRUMBS

1. **Mix together** an egg or two and some milk in a shallow, oblong bowl. Put breadcrumbs in a similar bowl.

2. **Submerge the meat,** one piece at a time, in the egg mixture. Let the excess drip off. Then roll each piece in the breadcrumbs.

FOR AN OVEN-FRIED CRUST WITH FLOUR

1. **Mix all-purpose flour** with seasoning in a shallow, oblong bowl. (One formula that works is ½ cup flour, 1 teaspoon salt, and ¼ to ½ teaspoon black pepper, tossed together.)

2. **Dredge the legs or thighs** in the seasoned flour, one at a time, until they're well coated.

ROASTING TURKEY LEGS, THIGHS, AND BREASTS

Advantages: Same as for roasting a whole chicken (see page 101)

STEPS TO TAKE

1. **Take the turkey** out of the fridge 45 to 60 minutes before roasting it. Pat it dry.

2. **Preheat the oven** to 450°F (230°C).

3. **Add butter and oil** (ideally in a 1:1 ratio) to the roasting pan.

4. **Wiggle the skin loose** on the legs and thighs (but don't remove it). Spread salt and pepper on the meat under the skin. Put the skin back in place. Or slice the skin loose along both sides of the breastbone, but don't remove the skin. Instead, work the seasoning under the skin of the breast, then smooth out the skin.

5. **Lay the turkey pieces,** skin-side up, in the roasting pan.

6. **Slather them all over** with oil or butter.

7. **Slide the turkey** into the oven. Immediately reduce the oven temperature to 350°F (180°C).

8. **Roast** for 15 to 20 minutes per pound, or until an instant-read meat thermometer inserted into the thickest part of the meat (but not against a bone) registers 150°F (66°C) (the USDA recommends 165°F/74°C).

9. **Let the meat rest** for 15 minutes before slicing.

DRESSING UP THE BIRD

Turkey takes well to seasonings and sauces:

- **Add rosemary and thyme** to the salt and pepper seasoning. Or replace the salt with garlic salt.

- **Drop onion wedges** and chunks of carrots and/or celery around the meat and roast them together.

- **Put apples or pears** and butternut or acorn squash slices, or sweet potato wedges, alongside the turkey before roasting.

- **Add ½ cup white wine** or orange juice to the roasting pan before putting it into the oven.

- **Top the meat** with a barbecue sauce, sweetened with molasses, for a change. Keep watch and tent the meat with foil if the sauce starts to darken too much before the turkey is tender.

ROASTING BEEF

Advantages: Same as for roasting a whole chicken (see page 101)

STEPS TO TAKE

1. **Preheat the oven** to 450°F (230°C).

2. **Salt and pepper** the meat generously on all sides. If you want to add any vegetables to the meat, do that now (see below).

3. **Place the meat** in the roasting pan, fat-side up, and slide it into the oven, uncovered. Roast for 15 minutes.

4. **Reduce the heat** to 325°F (170°C). Roast for 20 to 25 minutes per pound.

5. **Check the interior temperature** by inserting an instant-read meat thermometer through one side and well into the center of the meat. Remove the meat from the heat when the thermometer registers the desired temperature (see page 87).

6. **Let the meat rest** for at least 15 minutes before slicing or chunking it so it can absorb its juices. The meat will continue to cook for about 10 minutes after being removed from the heat.

IF YOU WANT TO ADD VEGETABLES . . .

- **Drop a collection** of sturdy vegetables, chunked, into the roasting pan around the beef before you start roasting. Don't forget cabbage wedges, along with the usuals—onions, carrots, celery, potatoes, leeks, and/or parsnips.

- **Add canned or stewed tomatoes** with or without their juice, a good handful of herbs, salt and pepper, and a cup or two of red wine or a few tablespoons of spirits to the pan before roasting.

- **If you're in a veggie mood,** 20 minutes or so before the end of the roasting time, toss in sliced fresh mushrooms, broccoli florets, green beans, chopped bell pepper, or asparagus pieces.

Instructions continue on page 110

WINE IS WONDERFUL.

If a recipe calls for ½ cup, use 2 cups. If you think the meat will be good in beef Burgundy, use the whole bottle! —JAY

IF YOU WANT TO ADD EVEN MORE FLAVOR . . .

1. **Shred the roasted beef** and send it into its glory by stirring chopped chipotles, cilantro, and black olives into the shredded meat. Or go in another direction and add chopped celery and onions, ketchup, barbecue sauce, vinegar, Worcestershire sauce, brown sugar, chili powder, and garlic powder to the shredded or chunked meat.

2. **Return the mixture** to the 325°F (170°C) oven and allow it to heat through for 20 to 40 minutes, depending on the quantity.

ROASTING PORK

Advantages: Same as for roasting a whole chicken (see page 101)

STEPS TO TAKE

1. **Preheat the oven** to 425°F (220°C), or 450°F (230°C) if you want a good burnish on the meat.

2. **Salt and pepper the meat** while the oven preheats. Or rub it with a mix of herbs and seasonings—maybe garlic powder, cumin, oregano, and cinnamon. Or rosemary, minced garlic, sugar, and cayenne. If you want to add any vegetables or other accompaniments to the meat, see Flavoring the Pork before Roasting (page 113).

3. **Sit the prepped roast** in a roasting pan or metal baking pan. Roast for 15 minutes.

4. **Reduce the heat** to 325°F (170°C). Pour in ½ cup wine, chicken broth/stock, or water. Cook low and slow for 1 hour 15 minutes to 1 hour 30 minutes, uncovered.

5. **Check every 15 to 20 minutes** to make sure the meat isn't cooking dry. Baste it with pan juices each time you check it. No pan juices? Add ¼ cup or so of liquid.

6. **Poke an instant-read meat thermometer** into the center of the meat (but without hitting a bone). The internal temperature should be between 140°F and 145°F (60°C and 63°C). If you're just a few degrees below that, remove the meat from the oven.

7. **Place the meat** on a plate and tent it with foil to keep it warm. Let it rest for 10 to 20 minutes so it can regather its juices before you slice the roast.

8. **Place the pan** over low heat on the stovetop and stir any browned bits loose from the bottom. If the pan is nearly dry, add wine, broth, or water to help loosen what's sticking. Let it cook down just until it's syrupy.

9. **Add some butter** to the pan drippings for a glossy finish. Pour over the sliced meat.

Instructions continue on page 113

FLAVORING THE PORK BEFORE ROASTING

- **Fruit and meat combinations** that play off each other heighten flavor. Pork takes to fruit—especially fresh or dried apples, pears, cherries, and apricots. It's also great with fresh or dried plums (pitted, of course). Drive up the sweetly acid flavor by adding cider or a fruity wine to the roasting pan. Scatter minced fresh or crystallized ginger over the meat and into the liquid. All these are in addition to giving the pork a healthy shower of salt and pepper before roasting.

- **Carnitas or pulled pork** may be calling your name. Use your best rub (see the suggestions in step 2 on page 111). When the meat is tender, shred it, mix it with orange juice and pan drippings, spread it out on baking sheets, and roast it at 400°F (200°C) until it is brown and crispy around the edges. Or run it under the broiler for a minute or so, watching to be sure it doesn't burn.

- **You can score the fatty side** of roast pork and stick sliced garlic cloves into the grooves before roasting. Or add sliced chiles and onions over the top and/or around the meat. Spoon in salsa, and squeeze the juice from a couple of fresh limes or lemons over the top before the meat goes into the oven. Pull the meat apart with two forks when it's done, and stir it and the sauce together. Toss on fresh cilantro to top it off.

BRAISING BEEF OR PORK

Advantages: Braising turns tougher or leaner cuts of meat into tender, flavorful eating. Brown the meat, add a flavorful liquid, then cook it low and slow for a tasty, succulent outcome.

STEPS TO TAKE

1. **Bring the meat** to room temperature. Rub the meat all over with a mix of salt and pepper, or add more seasonings, such as smoked paprika, ground ginger, crushed rosemary, or thyme.

2. **Sear the meat** (with a rub or not) on all sides in a skillet or Dutch oven if you have the time. Browning adds a level of flavor, but it's not essential.

3. **Preheat the oven** to 325°F (170°C).

Instructions continue on page 116

4. **Build some flavor** in the Dutch oven or a roasting pan before putting in the meat, if you like. Cook a bunch of sliced onions just until soft, season them with fresh or dried herbs, then nestle the meat on top. Or skip the onions and herbs and put the meat right into the pan.

5. **Add some flavor** on top of the meat, if that sounds good. Create a sauce—maybe horseradish, tomato paste, red wine, minced garlic, and chopped onions—to spread over the meat. Or skip this for a completely meaty flavor.

6. **Pour water** down the side of the pan so you don't wash off the rub or sauce. The liquid should come to about one-third the height of the meat.

7. **Cover the pan** and cook for 2 to 3 hours, depending on the size of the meat, or until the internal temperature is 145°F (63°C) and the meat pulls apart easily with the tug of a fork. If you want to add carrots, white or sweet potatoes, grape or cherry tomatoes, and/or other vegetables, put them in beside the meat about 1½ hours before the meat is finished.

8. **Pull the meat** into chunks or slice it across the grain. Mix the pieces into the broth (and vegetables) and serve.

STEWING BEEF OR PORK CUBES

Advantages: Stewing tenderizes and deepens the flavor of cubed, and often less expensive, meat in a simmering liquid without a lot of tending.

STEPS TO TAKE

MY WIFE AND I HAD OSSO BUCO at a fancy restaurant in Ann Arbor a few weeks after we were married. The next day a recipe for the dish was in the *New York Times Magazine*. So I made it, slavishly following the directions. Over time, though, I've substituted chicken for the veal; changed the emphasis to oregano, sage, and lemon; substituted rice for the potatoes; and added more wine. Now there's a whole continuum of osso buco in my mind, and measurements are gone! —JAY

1. **Bring the meat** to room temperature if you want to brown the beef or pork first. Then put 2 tablespoons or so of oil into a Dutch oven or large stockpot and heat over medium-high heat. Alternatively, preheat the Dutch oven or a roasting pan in the oven at 500°F (260°C).

2. **Stir in** the cubed beef or pork. Let brown until it's the shade you want, at least 2 to 3 minutes, stirring occasionally.

3. **Stir in** flour and brown some more.

4. **Add whatever hearty vegetables** and seasonings you want to cook with the meat cubes. Stir in enough stock to cover the meat and vegetables.

5. **Reduce the heat** on the stove to low, or reduce the oven temperature to 325°F (170°C). Cover and cook for 30 minutes.

6. **Add the more delicate vegetables,** if you're using any. Continue cooking for another 30 minutes or so, or until everything is as tender as you want but not overcooked.

7. **Taste.** Add more of whatever's needed.

8. **Stir in** tomato paste to deepen the flavor for a beef stew, or sour cream for pork stroganoff.

STEWING CHICKEN OR TURKEY LEGS OR THIGHS, OR A WHOLE CHICKEN

Advantages: Stewing tenderizes and deepens the flavor of large or whole pieces of meat because it fully immerses them in slow-simmering liquid. They require little supervision, just a check now and then for signs of tenderness—that the meat is pulling away from the bones or starting to separate.

STEPS TO TAKE

1. **Fill a stockpot** with enough water to cover the chicken or turkey pieces or a whole bird.

2. **Stir in** sliced carrots and onions, chopped celery, fresh parsley, salt, and pepper. Cover the pot and bring the water, vegetables, and seasonings to a boil.

3. **Add the meat** to the boiling water.

4. **Cover the pot,** reduce the heat, and simmer until the chicken or turkey is falling-off-the-bone tender but isn't overcooked, 30 to 60 minutes, depending on the quantity.

5. **Let the meat cool** in the stock.

6. **Lift out the chicken or turkey** and debone.

7. **Strain the stock.**

8. **Cut up the meat** and make pot pie or creamed chicken/turkey. Or add the meat to a salad or bowl or to enchilada sauce. Or scatter it over a pizza crust.

4 / SAUCES

SAUCES COMFORT, ENHANCE, RESCUE, EVEN COVER UP.
Sauces balance flavors, whether used with rich meats or quiet, unobtrusive grains.

Learn to recognize the possibilities right in front of you as you finish up a dish. (Always save the drippings!) Remember: Acids (wine, tomato and lemon juice, vinegar) wake things up.

Keep certain basics on hand so you can pull them into duty on a moment's notice—oil, vinegar, wine, lemons and limes, tomatoes in many forms, stock or broth, butter, fresh seasonings, honey, herbs. If you like to make sauces, set out several and let the people you're serving choose. Think:

- **What do you want the sauce to do?** I loved a sweet-sour sauce my mom added to chunks of leftover chuck roast. Now I realize she was stretching that meat into a second meal, which I happened to like better than the first round.

- **If you're imagining a flavorful sauce,** why not figure out what goes well with it? I've turned a butternut squash–apple soup into a mouthwatering pasta sauce. Another time, I added a little mustard to stewed apples, then spooned the mix over a ham steak.

- **Ready for some unexpected brightness in the middle of ordinary?** When green beans are in season and the garden won't relent, a sauce can bring magic to what's become boring. I soften a raft of chopped onions (or shallots or garlic) in butter, then let them sauté for a few minutes longer until the combination turns nutty brown. That, poured over the evening's green beans, lifts things. Sometimes a squeeze of lemon juice into the sauce feels right, too.

121

FREESTYLE COCONUT MILK CURRY

Serve this vegetable curry over rice, pasta, lentils, or potatoes.

INGREDIENTS THAT WORK WELL

- **coconut milk**
- **curry paste**
- **any vegetable** or combination of vegetables (cut into pieces)
- **onions**
- **garlic**
- **cooked meat**
- **ground cumin or cumin seeds**
- **rice, pasta, or potatoes**, for serving

How to Wing It

Stir together the coconut milk and curry paste in a large saucepan over medium heat.

Stir in the vegetables, onions, and garlic when the mixture begins to simmer.

Continue simmering until the vegetables are as tender as you like. Stir in the cooked meat, if using.

Taste. Stir in the cumin to get the flavor where you want it.

Serve over your choice of starch.

IF YOU LIKE CURRY AND ARE WILLING TO EXPERIMENT, you can add just about any vegetable to coconut milk simmered with curry paste. Just add the ingredients you're hungry for or are inclined to try. I used to be afraid of making curries, but I have found that just about anything will work if you start with those two ingredients! — EVONNE

FREESTYLE CLASSIC (MICROWAVED) WHITE SAUCE

INGREDIENTS THAT WORK WELL

- butter
- all-purpose flour
- milk
- salt and freshly ground black pepper

WHITE SAUCE IS A SUPER HELPER WITH LEFTOVERS. I love this microwave method because it doesn't need continuous attention and always works. You can add small pieces of chicken to it and pour it all over toast or roasted potatoes. Or stir in finely chopped, cooked veggies and spoon it over biscuits for breakfast. It's also easy to stir grated cheese into the white sauce, let it melt, then pour the cheesy sauce over pasta, with or without added cooked vegetables. —MARGARET

I get impatient waiting for a white sauce to thicken while I'm stirring it over a hot stove. I've tried reading while doing it, which helped. But I made the switch to the microwave when I was trying to hold a fussy child while also minding the white sauce. If you want a safe start, use these measurements to make 1¼ cups of white sauce: 2 tablespoons butter, 2 tablespoons flour, and 1 cup milk. The possibilities for its use are endless—combine it with leftover cooked vegetables and purée it as a soup, mix it with some hard-cooked eggs and place on top of toast, or use it to bring together vegetables and diced cooked chicken on top of biscuits. And that's just a start.

How to Wing It

Melt the butter by microwaving in a medium bowl on high for 1 minute.

Whisk in the flour. Microwave on high for 45 seconds.

Whisk in milk until the mixture is no longer lumpy. Microwave on high for 45 seconds. Whisk until smooth.

Continue heating in 45-second increments, then whisking, until the sauce is smooth and thickened.

Season to taste with salt and pepper.

HINTS FROM EUGENE

- **Use half-and-half instead of milk.** Hey, it's already a calorie train wreck, so why not go a little further.
- **Add grated cheddar,** Swiss, and Pecorino Romano cheeses, then finish with a grating of nutmeg.

MUSHROOM CREAM SAUCE

1. **Make a basic white sauce** (page 124), but before adding the flour, chop your favorite varieties of mushrooms, along with finely chopped onions, and sauté them in the butter.

2. **Stir in** the flour.

3. **Substitute crème fraîche** for some or all of the milk.

4. **To heat the sauce,** microwave on high in 45-second increments, whisking well between each increment, until the sauce is smooth and thickened.

5. **Stir in** truffle paste. Season to taste with salt and pepper.

6. **Serve immediately** over couscous or polenta, topping it with grated Parmesan cheese, if you want.

FRUITY WHITE SAUCE

1. **Make a basic white sauce** (page 124), but use mostly broth—vegetable or chicken—instead of milk. (If you use any milk, make sure it's whole and use just a smidge. The higher fat content will help prevent curdling.)

2. **Stir in grated ginger,** marmalade, white wine, and lemon or orange juice. Or use juice reserved from canned peaches, pears, or apricots.

3. **Serve over chicken and pasta** or rice. Or pour over sautéed or steamed vegetables.

ALFREDO SAUCE WITH WINE

1. **Make a basic white sauce** (page 124).

2. **Add about ¼ cup white wine** and stir till it's blended.

3. **Stir in** grated aged sharp cheddar cheese until it melts.

VEGAN ALFREDO SAUCE

1. **Soak cashews in water** to cover overnight, then drain and rinse. Alternatively, drain some tofu.

2. **Blend the drained cashews** or tofu for the base.

3. **Add nutritional yeast,** lemon juice, Italian seasoning, miso, and salt to taste.

CARBONARA

1. **Cook pancetta, lardons, or bacon** in a skillet over medium-high heat until it's as done as you like it—chewy or crispy.

2. **Add crème fraîche** or half-and-half to the meat and heat—without boiling—for 2 to 5 minutes, or just until the liquid warms. Keep watch. The amount of time depends on the quantity and whether the liquid was cold.

3. **Pour the sauce** over cooked pasta and stir it through. (Or make this a topping for cooked farro mixed with pieces of steamed asparagus. Or spoon it over a pizza crust before adding a smattering of lightly cooked broccoli and red onion slices.)

4. **Quickly add** a beaten egg, which will cook from the heat of the sauce and pasta and bind the carbonara together.

5. **Season to taste** with salt and pepper.

6. **Serve immediately** with grated Parmesan.

BLUE CHEESE SAUCE

1. **Break or cut** a chunk of blue cheese into small pieces.

2. **Melt the cheese** in a saucepan over low heat.

3. **Add half-and-half,** stirring continuously to blend and keep the sauce from sticking.

4. **Pour the sauce** over cooked pasta when the cheese is completely melted and the sauce is very warm. Or stir the sauce over a chicken-vegetable stew to brighten its flavor. Or ladle it over a platter of baked meatballs.

5. **Mix.** Season to taste with salt and pepper, if needed. Serve immediately.

Carbonara
over pappardelle pasta is a rich feast!

FREESTYLE TOMATO SAUCE

Serve this sauce over pasta or cooked grains, or use it to top a pizza, as a base for soup or stew, or to sauce a bowl.

INGREDIENTS THAT WORK WELL

- olive oil
- white onions (chopped)
- garlic (minced)
- an anchovy or two
- canned tomatoes
- tomato paste
- sugar
- basil
- oregano

START WITH ROMA TOMATOES, peeling and dicing them. Add about 1 cup olive oil to about 5 pounds tomatoes, along with chopped onions and garlic. Cook the mixture down in a saucepan, stirring frequently over low heat. Over time, the mixture emulsifies, creating an amazingly creamy and tomatoey sauce. —KYLE

HINTS

- **You can substitute fresh tomatoes for canned.** Consider using whole tomatoes with their skins on. Simply put them through a blender before adding them to the saucepan. The ground-up tomato skins make a sauce that isn't quite as smooth, but, hey, the blender treatment is way easier than peeling tomatoes. And we could all use a little extra fiber. —DARYL
- **If you need a tomato sauce but don't have tomatoes,** make a roasted red pepper sauce instead. —GINI

How to Wing It

Put oil, onions, garlic, and an anchovy or two in a saucepan.

Stir over medium heat until the anchovy disintegrates and the onions are translucent.

Crush tomatoes with your hands. Add to the saucepan.

Stir in a big spoonful of tomato paste and a little sugar.

Simmer the sauce until it cooks down and thickens to the consistency you want. Depending on the quantity, this will take 10 minutes to an hour.

Add basil and oregano to taste.

Taste again. Add whatever's missing.

ROASTED CHERRY TOMATO SAUCE

Roasted tomatoes add both richness and tartness to foods, and that depth of flavor is hard to replicate. I often use tomatoes to give body to dishes that have a good start and finish but need some help in the middle. Tomato juice or roasted tomatoes can often be the hidden ingredient that makes the difference in sauces, soups, and stews.

YOU MIGHT WANT TO ADD finely sliced or chopped carrots to the tomatoes. Or make a roasted carrot sauce by using finely sliced or chopped carrots instead of tomatoes in this recipe.

1. **Halve cherry tomatoes,** or rough-chop full-sized tomatoes (including those that are getting wrinkly and showing a few brown spots, which you can easily cut out).

2. **Mix the tomatoes** with a bit of olive oil, then spread them in a single layer on a greased baking sheet.

3. **Roast** in a preheated 400°F to 425°F (200°C to 220°C) oven for 5 to 10 minutes, or until the tomatoes blister and start to brown.

4. **Scrape the roasted tomatoes** into a bowl and stir vigorously, making a sauce of the broken-down veggies.

5. **Stir the tomatoes** into a pasta sauce or straight into cooked, warm pasta. Or spread them over a pizza base. Or spoon them over a bowl, partially filled with a base and other raw or cooked vegetables.

FREESTYLE PESTO

This beloved sauce is highly flexible. The traditional version includes a good-sized handful of a fresh flavorful herb, a pungent vegetable usually from the allium family, buttery nuts, punchy cheese, good olive oil, and seasonings. All are blended together until the mixture is relatively smooth and pourable.

How to Wing It

Chop the herbs and/or vegetables in a food processor.

Add cheese and nuts or seeds. Process until everything is well mixed.

With the food processor running, slowly drizzle in the oil through the feed tube. Process until the pesto is the consistency you like.

Season to taste with salt and pepper.

INGREDIENTS THAT WORK WELL

HERBS

- **basil** (roughly torn)
- **parsley** (chopped)

VEGETABLES

- **garlic** (minced)
- **beets** (diced and roasted)
- **broccoli** (steamed or sautéed lightly, cooled, and roughly chopped)
- **kale** (chopped)

CHEESE

- Parmesan

NUTS AND SEEDS

- pine nuts
- pumpkin seeds
- sunflower seeds
- walnuts

OIL

- olive oil

SEASONINGS

- lemon juice
- salt and freshly ground black pepper

BASIC BASIL PESTO

If you'd rather not waste your flavorful and beautiful basil on an experiment, here's a basic, traditional pesto recipe that you can count on.

INGREDIENTS

- 2 cups coarsely torn fresh basil leaves
- 2 garlic cloves, roughly chopped
- ½ cup freshly grated Parmesan cheese
- ¼ cup pine nuts or walnuts
- ½ cup olive oil
- Salt and freshly ground black pepper

STEPS TO TAKE

1. **Chop the basil** in a food processor.

2. **Add the garlic,** Parmesan, and nuts. Process until everything is well mixed.

3. **With the food processor running,** slowly drizzle in the oil through the feed tube. Process until the pesto is the consistency you like.

4. **Season to taste** with salt and pepper and blend briefly again, if needed.

ROASTED BEET PESTO

Here's a recipe that works for me, but alter it as you wish.

INGREDIENTS

- 1 large raw red beet
- 3 garlic cloves, chopped
- ¼ cup chopped walnuts
- ½ cup grated Parmesan cheese
- 2 tablespoons lemon juice
- ½ cup olive oil
- Salt and freshly ground black pepper

STEPS TO TAKE

1. **Peel and dice** the beet. Preheat the oven to 400°F (200°C).
2. **Wrap the beet pieces** in a foil packet. Lay the package in a baking pan to catch the juices.
3. **Roast** for 40 minutes, or until the beet is soft and juices are seeping out. Cool to room temperature.
4. **Combine** the roasted beet, garlic, walnuts, Parmesan, and lemon juice in a food processor. Process until well blended.
5. **With the food processor running,** slowly drizzle in the oil through the feed tube. Process until the pesto is the consistency you like. Add a little water if you'd like a more liquidy consistency.
6. **Season to taste** with salt and pepper.

MUSTARD SAUCE
OR VINAIGRETTE

This works as a sauce for rice and lentils or served alongside a pork roast. It can be used as a salad dressing, too. The typical ratio for a vinaigrette is 3:1—three parts oil to one part vinegar. Adding mustard and maple syrup to the vinegar yields a richer flavor, but the ratio stays the same.

1. **Place mustard,** white wine vinegar, and maple syrup into either a jar with a tight-fitting lid or a blender. Shake or blend together until well mixed.

2. **Add olive oil.** Shake vigorously or blend until thoroughly mixed and emulsified.

3. **Microwave** on high for 30 to 60 seconds, until warm, or use the sauce at room temperature.

TIPS FROM THE COOKING CIRCLE
MAKING SAUCES SING

- **Keep cans of coconut milk** and evaporated milk in your pantry to add a creamy finish to steamed spinach. Or add a tablespoon or two of balsamic vinegar or two dabs of tomato paste to sautéed Swiss chard. These ingredients give a slightly saucy character to the dish—and up the bright flavor.

- **Be careful not to overdo any additions.** The idea is to enhance the flavor of the original ingredients, not compete with them.

- **If you want a thicker or thinner sauce,** just decrease or increase the amount of liquid. If you've thinned the sauce, taste it to see if the flavor is diluted. If so, increase the seasonings a bit.

- **Use plain Greek yogurt and sour cream interchangeably,** as well as apple cider vinegar and lemon juice. —LINDSEY

- **Instead of pancake syrup,** melt butter and any jam or jelly you have over medium heat until it becomes pourable. Stir now and then as it heats to blend and keep it from sticking. My kids like the flavor it gives to pancakes. —BETH

MEDITERRANEAN SAUCE

Use this sauce to top burgers, sliced tomatoes, baked potatoes, or steamed or sautéed broccoli, asparagus, kale, spinach, or Swiss chard. And that's just a start.

1. **Place plain Greek yogurt** in a large bowl.

2. **Whisk in** olive oil until well blended.

3. **Gently stir** in grated cucumber, grated garlic, and lemon zest.

4. **Stir in** chopped fresh dill and mint.

5. **Add lemon juice,** salt, and pepper to taste.

6. **Taste again.** Add whatever seasoning is needed.

MY SUMMER SALSAS tend to be a cross between salsa and salad. I combine roughly equal amounts of green or red bell peppers and fresh tomatoes, chop one or two garlic cloves, then sprinkle on ground cumin, salt, freshly ground black pepper, and maybe some oregano. I drizzle olive oil and freshly squeezed lime juice over the vegetables and seasonings and stir everything together. If I want it spicy, I add a jalapeño or two. I usually serve this as a sauce to spice up the beans and rice that we eat almost daily for lunch.

—DARYL

How a Sauce Unfolds . . .

These are three of my favorite combinations:

- butter, garlic, walnuts, and thyme
- honey or agave syrup, vinegar of your choice, and soy sauce
- coconut milk and red curry paste

—EUGENE

I was melting a nice chunk of butter and a bit of pork lard in a cast-iron skillet. When the skillet was good and hot, almost smoking, I laid in the steaks. Then it was time to figure out what kind of sauce might go with the meat.

Brandy was starting to seem a little too sweet, so I was thinking of whiskey. I tried a taste of a brandy and two different whiskeys, and none was quite what I was looking for. Red wine was another option, and there was some left in a bottle in the fridge. My plan was shifting toward a more Provençal flavor as I realized that something red and tomatoey would go better on the yellow-white quinoa and grits that I was cooking to serve alongside the meat.

The steaks were just about done. After removing them from the skillet and setting them aside to rest, I deglazed the skillet and started the sauce.

I chopped a few capers that needed to be used up and tossed them into the skillet. In went a bit of wine to loosen things up, followed by a bit of parsley picked fresh from the garden.

Now garlic seemed necessary. I quickly chopped a clove and got it into the skillet, followed by a bit more wine because things were threatening to stick and burn.

This Provençal direction needed tomatoes, but I refuse to buy them out of season because they lack flavor, and I didn't want to open a can just for this . . . oh, but my wife always dehydrates several quart jars of tomatoes every summer. So I grabbed a handful, roughly chopped them, and let them reconstitute in the reducing wine. They would add a rich, deep, almost smoky tomato flavor and help the sauce reduce more quickly. In plopped a spoonful of coarse mustard, followed by vinegar from the capers and the juices that had collected under the resting steaks.

I soon turned off the heat and stirred in a bit more butter to make a silky but still a bit chunky sauce.

I put a scoop of quinoa and grits and a steak on each plate, ladled the sauce over both, then added Brussels sprouts and a big handful of pepper cress on the side. It all worked!

5 / BOWLS

YOU CAN MAKE A BOWL for any time of day (breakfast, lunch, dinner, snack). Intentional leftovers (a.k.a. "planned-overs"), such as cooked grains, cooked pasta, cooked potatoes, roasted vegetables, and salad dressings, are great for making bowls. Let some fresh fruit and vegetables accumulate for a few days, then think in layers when you assemble your bowl.

When you're feeding a group, assemble the bowls in whatever ways work best for you and the eaters. You can:

- **Pass all ingredients around the table.** You determine the order, starting with the most basic elements and ending with sauces and toppings. People choose what ingredients they want and how much.

- **Layer the basic ingredients** into individual bowls for everyone. Then pass additional ingredients so people can customize their own.

- **Set the ingredients in separate dishes** on the counter and invite people to build their own bowls, in whatever order and quantity they want.

BOWL-MAKING TIPS

- **Cook double or triple** the amount of grains you need at the moment. Stash the extras in meal-sized containers with tight-fitting lids and keep them within sight in the fridge. They're your route to quick meals for the rest of the week.

- **Try a variety of grains** so you and the people you cook for don't get tired of one grain. When you have several kinds, think about mixing them together to create a new bowl base.

- **For more flavor,** use broth or 100 percent juice (orange, apple, and tomato are especially flavorful) instead of water to cook dried grains.

- **Consider leftover vegetables or meats,** cheese ends, and a stray pear or apple (even those with some soft or brown spots) for your next bowl meal. Trim off any inedible parts and enjoy the flavorful parts that remain. They still have something to give to your meals.

- **Think color and texture** along with flavor and good nutrition when you plan a bowl. A dash of purple, red, or orange vegetables brightens up brownish grains and blond proteins. A few chopped nuts and chia seeds add a chewy bite to almost any bowl.

- **Flip forms.** Put burrito or fajita fillings into a bowl, swapping the tortilla for brown rice.

FREESTYLE COLD BREAKFAST

Layer 5
Yogurt (one flavor or several)

Layer 4
Torn fresh mint or
grated fresh ginger

Layer 3
Chopped nuts,
grated coconut,
or seeds

Layer 2
Chunked or sliced fresh or
canned fruit, berries,
or stewed apples

Layer 1
Any kind of granola, cooked
oatmeal, or dry oats (dry oats
soften up quickly when mixed
with fruit or swirled with a layer
of yogurt)

145
bowls

FREESTYLE HOT BREAKFAST

Layer 7
Sour cream, salsa, ketchup, or mustard

Layer 6
Avocado slices, fresh or dried herbs, or a mix of seasonings

Layer 5
Grated or sliced Gorgonzola, Romano, mozzarella, Parmesan, or feta cheese, alone or in combination

Layer 4
Chopped fresh or roasted tomatoes, chopped bell or hot pepper, or pickled anything that's compatible

Layer 3
Eggs—scrambled, poached, or fried

Layer 2
Crispy bacon, cooked ham slices or chunks, browned sausage slices or chunks, Canadian bacon, or browned tofu

Layer 1
Roasted potatoes—sweet or white, or a mixture (it's handy to have some planned-overs hanging out in the fridge)

146
bowls

FREESTYLE LIGHT ANYTIME MEAL

Layer 4

Salsa (corn and bean, tomato, pineapple, mango, or pico de gallo), tahini sauce, or a drizzle of maple syrup

Layer 3

Pepitas, sunflower seeds, or sesame seeds

Layer 2

Protein—cubed tofu, sliced cheese, grilled salmon or shrimp, a poached or sliced hard-cooked egg, scrambled eggs, omelet, or a few spoonfuls of beans

Layer 1

Variety of veggies—raw, cooked, or pickled; spiralized, sliced, or chunked (try sliced fresh or sautéed mushrooms and caramelized or pickled onions, mixed together for optimum texture and flavor)

147

bowls

FREESTYLE FRUIT BOWL

Layer 6
Cookie crumbs or chunks

Layer 5
Dollops of plain or vanilla Greek yogurt or frozen vanilla yogurt

Layer 4
Torn prosciutto or crumbled crispy bacon

Layer 3
Granola and/or chopped pecans or almonds

Layer 2
Berries and/or chopped or sliced peaches, watermelon, halved white or red grapes, plums, or mangoes

Layer 1
Cantaloupe or honeydew, halved and seeds removed to create two bowls

148
bowls

FREESTYLE MAIN MEAL

Layer 7
Sauce (tomato, cheese, oil and vinegar, peanut, buttermilk), yogurt and crushed fruit, creamy broth, pesto, or a poached egg

Layer 6
Chewy things—dried apple slices, whole cranberries or cherries, or cubed pineapple or mangoes

Layer 5
Crunchy things—seeds, nuts, or roasted chickpeas

Layer 4
Seasonal vegetables and/or fruit, raw or cooked—corn kernels, peas, tomatoes, green beans, spinach, berries, watermelon, pitted cherries, or sliced pome or stone fruits

Layer 3
Protein—beans of any kind, cooked or refried; chicken, turkey, pork, beef, salmon, tuna, shrimp, cooked and shredded, pulled, diced, or chunked; cubed tofu; or grated or cubed cheese of any variety

Layer 2
Cooked greens—asparagus, broccoli, cabbage, collards, or sugar snap peas

Layer 1
Cooked grain or seeds—rice, quinoa, wheat berries, farro—or cooked cubed, shredded, or mashed white and/or sweet potatoes (consider preparing a mixture of seeds and grains that cook the same length of time together: jasmine rice and bulgur, for example)

149
bowls

TILTING ASIAN

1. **Use a cooked rice base,** such as wild, brown, or jasmine, or whatever variety and texture you're hungry for.

2. **Add roasted pork,** cut up or shredded.

3. **Top with broccoli,** steamed or raw.

4. **Drizzle** peanut butter, tamari, or sesame oil with vinegar over the top.

5. **Finish** by sprinkling chopped peanuts and/or cilantro over everything.

THINKING HARVEST

1. **Use a spiralized sweet potato base,** cooked until fork-tender.

2. **Add browned ground turkey** or cut-up or shredded roasted turkey.

3. **Top with vegetables,** roasted or steamed.

4. **Add chopped celery,** minced red onions, and/or baby spinach.

5. **Pour heated bone broth** or gravy, pesto, or coconut milk over the top.

6. **Finish** with fresh orange segments, chopped apples, and/or dried cranberries.

MOSTLY MEDITERRANEAN

1. **Use a cooked pearl barley** or farro base, with fresh parsley or mint folded in.

2. **Add lightly cooked sea bass** or grouper and/or seared scallops.

3. **Top with tomatoes** (raw and sliced or roasted) along with finely sliced scallions or fennel bulb, snipped scallions, minced garlic, and/or asparagus tips (raw or sautéed).

4. **Add dollops of ricotta** or crumbled feta cheese.

5. **Pour vinaigrette** over the top.

Additional Sauce Ideas for Bowls

- barbecue sauce
- chicken, beef, or veggie stock (pages 208 and 212)
- favorite salad dressing
- harissa or tahini, mixed with stock for a saucy consistency
- pesto (page 135)

Korean Flavor Inspirations

Korean bibimbap is a real bowl inspiration. It's a great way to repurpose food, and I love the flavors.

The base of the dish is always glass noodles for me, although rice is more typical and quite good. The noodles sit at the bottom of the bowl. I think in quarters as I place food around the circle above the noodles. I start the first quarter with sautéed spinach or any other cooked vegetable from a previous meal. For the second quarter, I add something pickled like cucumber, carrots, onions, cabbage (kimchi is my favorite), ginger, or beets—whatever I have going on in the fridge. In the next quarter, I place chicken or fish from dinner the night before or turkey bacon from breakfast, sliced or shredded. For the last quarter, I add any Asian sauce I can find in the fridge. I usually use a black soybean sauce with chiles.

Finally, I poach or fry an egg and place it in the middle on top of everything. I'm careful to keep the yolk runny so that when it breaks, it runs down through the dish.

This bowl brings in salty, earthy, sour, and spicy flavors. The textures are varied but complement each other. It all makes for an exciting meal. And it's nutritionally balanced with vegetables, proteins, and starches.

This is what can happen with a bunch of leftovers and staples from the fridge!

BROWN RICE AND TOFU BUDDHA

1. **Use a cooked brown rice base** livened up with minced garlic and/or fresh ginger, torn fresh basil, or a few spoonfuls of vinaigrette or a creamy yogurt dressing amped up with Sriracha sauce, if you want some sting.

2. **Add cubed, browned tofu** or some combination of seitan, tempeh, lentils, edamame, or cooked egg.

3. **Top with thin carrot** and zucchini sticks, steamed or raw.

4. **Add steamed broccoli florets** and sliced mushrooms.

5. **Pour more vinaigrette** (flavored with soy sauce, rice vinegar, honey, and minced ginger and garlic) or a creamy yogurt dressing, with or without Sriracha sauce, over the top.

6. **Add spoonfuls of sesame seeds** (toasted or raw), chopped nuts, or roasted chickpeas.

7. **Finish** by sprinkling chopped fresh mint, parsley, or oregano over the top.

AEGEAN CHICKEN AND CHICKPEAS

1. **Use a cooked quinoa** or orzo base or a mixture of the two for an interesting texture.

2. **Add sliced, cooked chicken** breasts or thighs, fanned over the top.

3. **Top with chickpeas,** chopped fresh tomatoes, sliced cucumbers, chopped fresh spinach, thinly sliced red onions, avocado cubes, or a handful of fresh parsley.

4. **Sprinkle on crumbled feta cheese** or sliced black olives.

5. **Add spoonfuls of hummus** here and there over the surface, or set an entire hummus container in the center of the bowl if you're filling a large bowl to be shared.

6. **Squeeze lemon wedges** over the top.

Steak
Goes to
Asia

STEAK GOES TO ASIA

1. **Use rice noodles**—cooked, well rinsed, and drained—as a base.

2. **Add thin slices** of grilled beef or pork.

3. **Top with shredded lettuce,** thinly sliced cucumbers, your favorite sprouts, or cilantro leaves.

4. **Sprinkle chopped peanuts** and sliced scallions over the top.

5. **Pour fish sauce**—your own, or store-bought from a good Asian food market—over everything.

POKE BOWL

1. **Use a base of cooked grain,** white or brown short-grain rice, soba noodles, spiralized zucchini, or hearty raw greens (torn-up kale, chard, spinach, and/or romaine).

2. **Add cooked ahi tuna** (thinly sliced or cubed), salmon (fresh or smoked), crabmeat, shrimp, or snapper.

3. **Top with sliced avocado,** seaweed, pickled chopped vegetables, diced scallions, julienned carrots, skinny cucumber sticks or slices, and thinly sliced radishes.

4. **Sprinkle on sesame seeds** (plain or toasted) and/or a light shake of sea salt (pink, if you like).

5. **Pour a sauce** that partners well with fish—wasabi or hot sauce for some heat, soy sauce and rice vinegar for a vinaigrette, plain yogurt with a minced hot pepper and grated ginger for a creamy touch—over the top.

6. **Finish with fresh herbs** parsley, oregano, or sliced strips of basil.

RICE AND BEANS BOWL

1. **Fill two-thirds** of a large serving bowl with cooked rice and beans (see Margaret's Flavorful Cooked Beans, facing page), warm or at room temperature.

2. **Add a touch of hot sauce** if the people eating enjoy it. (Keep the bottle on the table for those who want more.)

3. **Top** with torn fresh garden spinach, guacamole, spicy salsa, cilantro, and grated smoked cheese.

4. **Make a vinaigrette** with lime juice and vinegar, mixed with olive oil and flavored with mustard and honey, or make a creamy dressing with a sour cream and mayo start and then some ketchup, Worcestershire sauce, salt, freshly ground black pepper, garlic powder, and ground cumin stirred in.

5. **Pour the dressing** over the top, or let people add their own.

Margaret's Flavorful Cooked Beans

These are perfect in a rice and beans bowl (see facing page).

Pour dried black beans and twice as much water into a slow cooker (I usually make 2 cups of dried beans at a time). Cook on low or high until soft. Depending on the age of the beans, this could take anywhere from 2 to 5 hours. You can soak the beans ahead of time if you remember. Once they're cooked, let them sit in their liquid until you're ready to use them later in the day. Freeze whatever beans you're not using immediately in their liquid.

When you're ready to prep the cooked beans for eating, sauté an onion in oil or bacon fat over medium-high heat, in either a heavy skillet or a cast-iron Dutch oven. Add these seasonings to the onion as it sautés: dried oregano, chili powder, ground cumin, salt, sugar, and freshly ground black pepper. Taste to make sure you have the balance right.

When the onion is sizzling soft, reduce the heat to medium-low and stir in the cooked beans and their liquid. Use a potato masher to mash the beans roughly, aiming to crush about half of them. Let the whole business simmer, uncovered, until the liquid is reduced.

Taste occasionally. Add more oregano, cumin, or chili powder if you want more flavor. Don't add more salt until the very end—if it's needed at all—because the beans are getting concentrated and it's easy to oversalt at this point. Continue cooking the beans until they're as soupy or dry as you like—or until you're out of time. Mix the beans and their juice with cooked rice and ladle into a big bowl or smaller individual bowls. Set out additional toppings and call the gang to the table.

BEEF NACHO BOWL

1. **Use torn-up corn tortillas** or nachos as a base.

2. **Add cooked sausage** or ground beef.

3. **Top with sweet corn** (cooked or raw), chopped onions, bell and/or hot peppers, and black beans.

4. **Finish** with hot sauce, shredded sharp cheese, guacamole, and chopped cilantro for topping.

STORIES FROM THE COOKING CIRCLE: **LEE**

Before There Were Bowls, There Were Casseroles

Once upon a time, someone shared a recipe with us for a dish called Beef Nacho Casserole. The basic setup was ground beef, sweet corn, and a mayo and salsa mixture, alternating with layers of corn tortillas and cheese. As a casserole, it's relatively quick and tasty and can be easily scaled up for a large group.

Over the years of making this dish, I've substituted yogurt for mayo and sausage for beef, and I've added black beans and chopped onions and peppers, among other adjustments. Of course, we've also learned to serve it with hot sauce, guacamole, and cilantro.

I don't bother with a recipe. I know what I'll start with, then I add to that depending on what's in season. This way of cooking is fairly common in our house.

"WHAT GROWS TOGETHER GOES TOGETHER" BOWL

Vegetables that are harvested during the same months of the year often have compatible flavors. They can be good company to each other in a bowl.

1. **Use roasted, cubed root vegetables**—such as potatoes, carrots, or beets—as a base.

2. **Add seasonings**—salt, freshly ground black pepper, minced garlic, pickled onions, and/or a spoonful or two of kimchi.

3. **Top with vegetable cousins**—roasted or steamed cauliflower or broccoli florets and their cut-up stems, and roasted or steamed thinly sliced cabbage wedges.

4. **Add a handful of raw vegetables**—grated carrots, finely chopped shallots, broken cauliflower and broccoli florets, or chopped cabbage.

5. **Add orange zest,** topped with a handful of fresh orange segments spread across the cooked vegetables.

6. **Make a vinaigrette** with fresh orange juice and apple cider vinegar, shaken together with extra-virgin olive oil in a jar with a tight-fitting lid, then seasoned with chopped tarragon, a bit of sea salt, and several grinds of black pepper. Taste. If it's not bright, add more orange juice and shake again.

7. **Pour the vinaigrette** over the top of the bowl.

8. **Finish** with a sprinkle of chopped walnuts (toasted, if you have the time and inclination) just before serving.

OCEANSIDE BOWL
FOR SHARING

1. **Use a base of cooked rice**—wild, brown basmati, or white long-grain

2. **Add a spoonful or two of dressing**—olive oil, lime juice, soy sauce, and finely chopped or grated fresh ginger.

3. **Massage a pile of torn kale leaves** with a couple tablespoons of vinaigrette for a minute or two. Add the massaged kale and some fresh spinach to the rice base.

4. **Top** with a good-sized seared salmon fillet (see page 97).

5. **Place avocado slices** and fresh pear or mango slices over the top.

6. **Finish** with more spoonfuls of dressing. Bring any remaining dressing to the table so eaters can add more if they want.

6 / SALADS

WHATEVER YOU PUT IN YOUR SALAD has a right to be noticed: the base (greens, grains, seeds, pasta), each vegetable, every cube of fruit, the protein, and the crunchy and the creamy elements.

Use a big bowl to mix the salad so you're focused more on what you're adding than on keeping the ingredients from hopping out as you toss. Then keep the following in mind:

- **What texture do you want?** What texture will each of your ingredients give to the whole?

- **What flavors are you after?** How will each flavor you add affect the whole?

- **Think construction.** Build the salad so there's a piece of each ingredient in every bite.

- **Dress the salad as you go.** Every element should have a glance of dressing.

- **Place the heaviest ingredients on the bottom** and the lightest on top. Or build a salad in repeating layers (base, heavier items, lighter items, dressings, repeat), no tossing required.

FREESTYLE VEGETABLE-BASED SALADS

INGREDIENTS THAT WORK WELL

FRESH VEGETABLES

Use a mixture of chunked fresh vegetables (especially good when local gardens are growing).

- broccoli
- Brussels sprouts
- cabbage
- carrots
- cauliflower
- celery
- corn kernels
- cucumbers
- kale or chard (sliced into ribbons)
- mushrooms
- peppers (bell or hot; of all colors)
- red onions
- sprouts
- squash
- tomatoes

COOKED VEGETABLES

Use steamed, roasted, or grilled vegetables (good any time of year).

- any of the fresh vegetables mentioned at left, except cucumbers and sprouts
- beets
- green beans
- potatoes

NUTS AND SEEDS

Think both flavor and texture.

- almonds (sliced)
- cashews
- flax seeds
- hazelnuts
- macadamia nuts
- pecans
- pepitas
- pine nuts
- poppy seeds
- sesame seeds
- sunflower seeds

SINGLE VEGETABLE

Use any one of these— cooked or raw, leftover or fresh—as a main ingredient.

- beets (chunked)
- broccoli (chopped)
- carrots (steamed)
- corn
- green beans

FRESH HERBS

Use a handful.

- cilantro
- dill
- oregano
- sage
- tarragon
- thyme

HARD-COOKED EGGS

Use halved or chopped.

CHEESE

Use cubed, shredded, or sliced.

- mozzarella (fresh)
- paneer
- Swiss cheese

SEASONINGS

- black pepper
- dried herbs
- salt

DRESSINGS

- creamy dressing
- lemon juice
- salsa
- vinaigrette

HINTS

Don't automatically throw out any fresh veggies that have a few brown spots or are going soft in places. Just cut out the inedible parts and dispose of them. Keep the good parts for your vegetable salad.

A vegetable-based salad can make a full meal if you add grains or pair it with seared chicken or pork.

Look in the freezer for peas. There's no need to thaw them; just break them up as you mix them into the salad.

Serve the salad cold or at room temperature.

169
salads

How to Wing It

Pull out the vegetables (leftover or fresh) from your fridge and survey what you have.

See what's in your pantry if you want more vegetables. Include a single variety of canned beans, or many kinds (drained and rinsed). If tomatoes aren't in season, add diced canned tomatoes (reserving the juice for the dressing); they're a lot more flavorful than out-of-season fresh ones. Consider canned beets (drained). They'll add flavor, and likely a tinge of pink to the whole mix.

Start chunking the vegetables. Add them fresh to the mixing bowl as you finish, or roast or sauté them (see page 35 for vegetables that roast and sauté well). If you cook the vegetables, let the pan drippings cool, then scrape them into the salad to keep all that good flavor.

Add additional ingredients that you think will fit and add flavor. How about those steamed green beans or asparagus in the fridge? Top them with finely chopped red onion and hard-cooked eggs, then drizzle them with a light vinaigrette.

Season to taste. Add seasonings, a bit at a time, continuing to taste as you go.

Consider which dressing, if any, will enhance the vegetable flavors. Stir fresh basil, oregano, and minced garlic into a mixture of olive oil and lemon juice. Blend well, then stir in grated Parmesan cheese. Pour over fresh tomatoes and leafy greens. Fresh dill and chives, blended with mayo, mustard, and lemon juice, work well with chunked cucumbers. Or pour that creamy mix over steamed asparagus or zucchini matchsticks. Or start with olive oil and red wine vinegar, then stir in whatever's fresh in your herb pots—tarragon, chives, parsley. Spin in some mayo and drizzle it over a medley of chickpeas and chopped red onions on a big plate of arugula. Or stir in some reserved tomato juice from canned tomatoes . . .

Marinate leftover steamed veggies in a vinaigrette and arrange them as a salad or serve them as a pickle.

—MARGARET

A Quick Spring Sunday Lunch

I spent most of Saturday in the yard and garden. There was no time to invite guests for lunch after church. But on Sunday morning, in the warmth of community, I invited a young couple over to join us for lunch after the service. It was okay with them if the house wasn't perfect. I figured that whatever we pulled together to eat would be fine. The point was the conversation and the fellowship, yet, as always, I wanted the meal to sing.

At church, a retired couple had brought fresh asparagus from their garden and made it available to anyone who gave a donation to the youth group. So then we had asparagus. I asked myself what else I could pull together quickly so that things were mostly ready when the guests arrived.

HERE'S WHAT I HAD ON HAND:

- nice bunch of asparagus
- ripe avocado
- variety of greens from our spring garden: radishes, cilantro, scallions
- several limes and olive oil
- fresh loaf of crusty rye bread
- little bits of a variety of cheeses: tangy blue, Brie, sharp aged cheddar, hard goat, and baby Swiss

I sliced some bread and set the slices on a cutting board in the middle of the table along with the cheeses, which were coming up to room temperature. This gave the guests something to nibble while I prepared the rest of the meal.

To make a dressing with Mexican flavors, I combined the juice of two limes, olive oil, salt and pepper, minced scallions including the white parts, and minced cilantro, which I tossed gently with avocado slices.

The trimmed asparagus went into a skillet over medium heat with a bit of olive oil, where the spears sautéed for a few minutes. To serve, we passed the greens first, followed by the warm asparagus and the avocado dressing. We had radishes, still small that early in spring, on the table for sprinkling on top by those who wanted them. People combined the ingredients in whatever way they liked.

My wife informed the guests that the little tidbits of cheese had to be used up before the meal was over, because they were not going back in the fridge!

FREESTYLE LEAFY GREEN SALADS

INGREDIENTS THAT WORK WELL

FRESH GREENS

Use one variety or a mixture, chopped or torn, as a base. The base makes up about one-half to one-third of the volume of the total salad.

- endive
- lettuce, such as red and green leaf
- romaine lettuce
- spinach
- watercress

OTHER FRESH VEGETABLES

Use chopped, cubed, or sliced.

- avocado
- bell peppers
- broccoli
- carrots
- cauliflower
- celery
- corn kernels
- cucumbers
- mushrooms
- onions
- peas
- radishes
- sprouts
- tomatoes

COOKED VEGETABLES

Use steamed, roasted, grilled, or canned (and drained) vegetables, at room temperature or chilled.

- asparagus
- bell peppers
- broccoli
- Brussels sprouts
- carrots
- cauliflower
- eggplant
- mushrooms
- potatoes (white and sweet)
- zucchini

FRUIT

Use fresh, dried, or canned (with juice reserved for dressing), chopped, cubed, or sliced.

- apple and pear slices (no need to peel)
- apricots
- bananas
- blueberries
- cantaloupe
- grapes (red and white; halved)
- honeydew
- mangoes
- oranges
- peaches
- pineapple
- plums
- strawberries
- watermelon

DARK LEAFY GREENS

To soften, salt the separated leaves liberally, then massage the salt into the leaves. Yep, with your hands. When you feel the leaves yielding, you can stop.

- cabbage
- collards
- kale

PROTEINS

- eggs (hard-cooked)
- lentils (cooked)
- meat (cooked and chopped or cubed)
- nuts
- soybeans (cooked or dry-roasted)
- tofu or tempeh (cubed)

BREAD CHUNKS with GOOD TEXTURE

- croutons
- stale sturdy bread . . . how about panzanella?
- toasted pita

FRESH HERBS

Use chopped or torn.

- basil
- cilantro
- dill
- mint
- oregano
- parsley
- rosemary

CHEESE

Use grated, cubed, broken, or crumbled.

- Asiago
- blue
- cheddar
- Cotija
- feta
- goat
- Gruyère
- Parmesan
- pepper jack
- Romano

SEASONINGS

- garlic (minced)
- ginger (grated)
- harissa
- herbs (dried)
- miso
- salt and freshly ground black pepper
- sumac
- tahini
- za'atar

DRESSINGS

- apple cider vinegar and olive oil with mustard, salt and black pepper, garlic and onion powders, and fresh herbs
- lemon juice and honey with herbs and seasonings

Cooked, chunked sweet potatoes work well over greens.

Always have an avocado on hand.

Set out a variety of dressings so eaters can choose their own.

HINTS

- **Decide which elements *you* will add to the salad** and which elements you're going to let *the eaters* choose to add. Letting people customize their salad increases the chances of pleasing everyone at the table. Put some of the ingredients into smaller serving bowls, along with spoons, and pass them after everyone's been served the salad basics.

- **Consider offering a variety of dressings.** Again, everyone gets to choose his or her own.

YOU CAN USE VIRTUALLY ANY LEFTOVER AS PART OF A SALAD.
Dice up yesterday's cold vegetables (including potatoes), meat, and leftover cheese, toss everything in a vinaigrette, maybe put a fried egg on top, and you have a whole new meal. —CHRISTINA

How to Wing It

Gather everything that you want to chop, cube, or slice. Think about how dominant you want each ingredient to be in the final mix. That will affect the size of the pieces you make and how much of each ingredient you'll cut up.

Place the greens in the bowl If you'll be eating soon, then add each prepped ingredient as you finish with it. If you'll be eating later, place the prepped food, either separately or together, into containers with lids. Refrigerate until needed.

Toss together the ingredients you want to feature as the main part of the salad just before serving.

Put the other ingredients into individual serving dishes so each person can choose whether or not to add them to the salad.

Set out the dressings in bowls with a spoon for each type.

Handheld Salads

Why not wrap up a spoonful of those vegetables and their extras in good-sized Boston lettuce or romaine leaves? Keep the chunks of veggies fairly small so they don't punch through the leaves. Plus small pieces allow for a greater mixture in each package.

1. Lay out the lettuce leaves and open each one wide. Center a spoonful of salad ingredients from side to side on the lower half of the leaf.

2. Drizzle lightly with dressing.

3. Fold in both sides of the leaf. Fold the bottom up over the salad ingredients, then roll up. Count on making four or more leaf packages for each serving.

MAKING GREAT SALADS

- **Always have fresh greens** or a bagged salad and an avocado on hand. A Caesar salad as a side to meat is just about perfect. An avocado will hold for a week in the fridge after it starts to get soft. A few slices of fresh avocado on top of salad greens, or fanned out as a side with a little vinaigrette or lemon juice spooned over them, is very satisfying. —LORRE

- **Cooked and cooled sweet potatoes, chunked or sliced,** work well over greens for a salad. Add toasted nuts, dried cranberries, and feta cheese, all to top things off color- and flavor-wise. —BETH

- **Try to understand what each ingredient is doing in the recipe.** That helps you figure out what you can substitute without losing any flavor or texture. You might use cucumber as the crunchy green element in potato salad in summer instead of celery if celery only grows locally in spring and fall. Don't be afraid to swap the kind of cheese that's specified in a recipe. See if it's a mild or a sharp cheese that's called for, and go with what you have on hand that's similar. —MARGARET

- **Keep track of extra-fresh foods on the counter and in the fridge**—they're the "won't keep much longer" vegetables. In summer, put them in a massive green salad, pasta salad, or rice salad. In winter, put them in soups. —EVONNE

- **Complex salads are a great way to round out a meal.** Avocado slices, walnuts, fresh pear chunks, citrus segments without skin or membrane, cannellini beans—these can fill nutritional gaps. If you're wondering what to serve with eggplant Parmesan, consider a big, complex salad that includes several types of greens, along with fruit, vegetables, and often some nuts. —EUGENE

- **Cook from your imagination and memory.** I started making chicken salad the other day. I thought, *Apples are good with chicken. Cinnamon goes with apples. Honey goes with both—and with raisins and cranberries*. I brought everything together, along with some chopped celery and mayonnaise, and served it on a bed of fresh greens. They all fit—the flavors, the colors, and the textures. —BETH

Zahra shared these great ideas:

- **Start your meals with a salad or vegetable course.** Kids especially like ants on a log (celery sticks spread with peanut butter, with raisins perched on top) and carrots with hummus. People of any age will eat sliced cucumbers with pink salt, roasted beets with dollops of yogurt, or stir-fried garlicky broccoli. Let kids and adults alike fill up on those as you finish the meal.

- **Hold back the big protein** and bring everyone to the table for conversation and the first round of food. Then bring on the protein, followed by baguettes with butter or balsamic vinegar. Always include fats to help slow down the energy release from the carbs.

farro

wheat berries

wild rice

white rice

barley

quinoa

brown rice

Kamut

steel-cut oats

freekeh

FREESTYLE GRAIN OR PASTA SALADS

INGREDIENTS THAT WORK WELL

COOKED GRAINS

Keep a supply in the fridge or cook grains the day or evening before you want to use them so they're cooled when you need them.

- barley
- bulgur
- farro
- freekeh
- Kamut
- oats (steel-cut)
- quinoa
- rice
- wheat berries

COOKED PASTA

Make pasta on the spot if you have time. Or precook it so it's ready for salad making as soon as you are. Or use leftover pasta, if that ever happens in your kitchen.

- orzo
- ramen noodles
- rice vermicelli
- rotini
- soba noodles

BEANS

Use canned or your own precooked beans.

- black beans
- chickpeas
- Great Northern beans

FRESH VEGETABLES

- asparagus (broken into pieces)
- avocado (chunked)
- broccoli florets
- corn kernels
- green beans (broken into pieces)
- mushrooms (sliced)
- onions of any color (thinly sliced or chopped)
- peas
- peppers (chunked or diced)
- radishes, cucumbers, celery (sliced)
- scallions (thinly sliced or chopped)
- spinach leaves (finely torn)
- sugar snap peas (sliced)
- tomatoes (chopped)

STEAMED, ROASTED, or SAUTÉED VEGETABLES

Stash these in the fridge, or if you have time to cook now, see chapter 1 for instructions about how to steam, roast, or sauté veggies.

- broccoli
- corn
- green beans
- onions
- potatoes (cooked and diced)
- summer or winter squash
- zucchini (sliced)

GRILLED MEAT

Use chopped or shredded meats.

- chicken
- pork
- tuna

OTHER PROTEINS

- eggs (hard-cooked)
- lentils

CHEESE

- blue
- cheddar
- feta
- Gorgonzola
- Parmesan
- queso blanco

DRESSINGS

Use quiet or zesty, depending on the other flavors in the salad.

- mayonnaise-based dressing
- salsa
- vinaigrette
- yogurt-based dressing

EXTRAS

- artichoke hearts (chopped)
- black or green olives (sliced)
- fresh herbs (by the handful; chopped)
- raisins and/or other dried fruits
- sprouts
- sun-dried tomatoes (chopped)

NUTS AND SEEDS

Chop and toast, then spoon these over the top after you've done the final toss of the salad ingredients. This will keep them from sinking to the bottom of the bowl, where they're likely to be missed by most who are eating.

HINTS

- **Rinse uncooked quinoa** under cold water before cooking it to wash off the natural coating that can otherwise result in bitterness.

- **Consider a vinaigrette dressing** that will kick up a little tempest of flavor when mixed with an earthy grain. It's best if the dressing flavor doesn't dominate, but it can wake things up a bit.

ADD COOKED AND COOLED WHEAT BERRIES AND FARRO to salads to make the salad a main dish. Grains are so mild mannered that they work with just about any kind of dressing you want to use . —DARYL

How to Wing It (Grain Salads)

Bring the raw grain and liquid to a boil. Reduce the heat so the mixture simmers. Cover and cook for the time indicated in the charts on pages 76–77.

Stir in chopped or sliced onions or scallions while the grain is still warm.

Add several glugs of your favorite vinegar and several pinches of salt.

Fluff and stir everything together with a fork. Taste. Add whatever seasonings you want, and more vinegar, if needed. Cover the mix and let it cool to room temperature.

Stir in several tablespoons of olive oil to loosen up the grain.

Add fresh, cooked, canned, and/or roasted veggies; grated or cubed cheese; bite-size cooked meat, if you wish; chopped fresh herbs; and dried fruit.

Top the salad with nuts and seeds after the last toss so they don't sink to the bottom of the bowl.

Taste before serving. If something seems to be missing, add another splash or so of vinegar and maybe some coarsely ground black pepper.

TIPS FROM THE COOKING CIRCLE
CONSTRUCTING A FLAVORFUL SALAD

Evonne shared these great ideas:

- Make a salad visually appealing. Use a rainbow of ingredients if possible.

- Prepare ingredients in a way that brings out the most flavor (for example, decide whether to roast or steam vegetables).

- Add enough liquid and seasonings to make sure the end product will not be dry or bland.

- Taste and adjust, taste and adjust, taste and adjust.

Top with nuts at the end, so they don't sink to the bottom.

Add chopped fresh vegetables and herbs after you fluff the cooked grain.

Consider flavor as well as texture when adding elements.

Use short, twisty pasta that will catch other ingredients.

HINTS

- **Go with short, twisty pasta** with nooks and crannies that will catch the other ingredients you plan to add. (Long, slippery pasta strands let the added ingredients slide to the bottom of the serving bowl and your dinner plate.)
- **Don't rinse the pasta after it's cooked.** The starchy coating on the drained noodles will help the dressing—as well as smaller added ingredients—stick.
- **Stir plenty of dressing** into the cooked pasta while it's warm. Then it can soak up some of the dressing, adding flavor and tenderness to the pasta.

How to Wing It (Pasta Salads)

Cook the pasta if you don't have already-cooked pasta on hand. Drain and let cool for 2 minutes.

Stir in the dressing. If you're starting with already-cooked pasta, stir in the dressing gently but firmly, breaking up any clumps of pasta as you go.

Wash and dry the vegetables if they're raw. Take cooked vegetables out from the fridge, or break open a can or two from your pantry (drain the cans). Cut, slice, or break the vegetables.

Stir in the dense vegetables.

Decide what else you want to add, considering flavor and texture: chopped or shredded cooked meat? Crumbled or sliced cheese?

Stir in the meat and/or cheese.

Set out any extras you're considering adding.

Stir in the delicate vegetables and extras just before serving.

185
salads

Leftover grilled lemon chicken will make a terrific chicken salad. Add mayonnaise, grapes, and chopped nuts, and stuff it all into a lettuce leaf. No one remembers you served the chicken 3 days ago at dinner. Cooked salmon works equally well. —CHRISTINA

FREESTYLE PROTEIN SALADS

Enjoy these salads on greens or breads.

INGREDIENTS THAT WORK WELL

MEAT, SEAFOOD, and EGGS

- chicken or turkey (grilled)
- clams (cooked)
- eggs (hard-cooked or jammy)
- mussels (cooked)
- pork tenderloin (roasted)
- salmon or white-fish fillets (flaked or chopped)
- shrimp (grilled; whole or chopped)
- steak or scallops (broiled)
- tuna (cooked)

RAW VEGETABLES

- carrots (grated)
- celery
- onions
- peppers (bell or hot)
- scallions
- tomatoes

COOKED VEGETABLES

- asparagus (steamed)
- beets (steamed or roasted; added just before serving)
- broccoli florets (steamed)
- chickpeas
- corn
- green beans (steamed or roasted)
- peas
- white beans

FRUIT

Use chopped, raw or dried.

- apples
- apricots
- blueberries
- cranberries
- grapes
- oranges
- pineapple
- raisins
- strawberries

COOKED PASTA AND GRAINS

LEAFY GREENS

- arugula
- baby spinach
- Boston, red leaf, and romaine lettuce
- endive
- kale
- Swiss chard

CHEESE

Use shredded, chopped, or sliced. What part do you want the cheese to play—mild and creamy, or punchy and noticeably present? Choose accordingly.

- cheddar
- feta
- Gorgonzola
- mozzarella (fresh)
- provolone

NUTS

- almonds (sliced)
- cashews (halved or broken)
- pecans (halved or broken)

DRESSINGS

- light oil and vinegar or citrus juice
- mayo- or yogurt-based dressing that won't overwhelm the flavor of the meat

SEASONINGS

- capers
- fresh herbs (chopped)
- salt and freshly ground black pepper
- whatever else will enhance the combination of ingredients you've brought together

HINTS

Think about whether you'll be spooning your protein salad over torn lettuce or other leafy greens or eating it in potato rolls or on top of toast. That may help you decide which dressing you want and how much to use.

Do you want to make this a sandwich melt? Think about that before you choose the cheese and its form.

187
salads

**ANYTIME YOU
GRILL MEAT,** make
extra to use for lunch
salads the next day.
Put the meat on top of
greens and add hard-
cooked eggs, carrots,
and whatever other
fresh vegetables are in
season. Since the meat
and its seasoning vary
depending on what
you've made the day
before, the salads won't
get monotonous.

—LINDSEY

How to Wing It

Chop the cooked meat, seafood, or hard-cooked eggs. If you want the
flavor to be dominant, keep the chunks fairly sizable. If you want the protein
to fit quietly into the salad along with vegetables, fruit, or pasta, make the
pieces smaller.

Cut up the other ingredients, keeping in mind their part in the salad and
how big they should be. Put them in the serving bowl.

Choose the dressing and gently mix it in.

Taste and decide what seasoning is needed. Start by adding a small amount
in one corner of the salad. If you like it, add more and stir it into the whole.

Place the meat, seafood, or chopped egg on top of the salad. Or mix it into
the salad and stuff the salad into buns. Or broil cheese-topped open-face
meat salad sandwiches.

From Lorre

QUICK, FRESH SALAD FOR A CROWD

I made this salad recently in about 10 minutes for 30 real estate agents from along Florida's beautiful Emerald Coast. If you need to do something similar, start with a big bowl!

1. Place a 28-ounce bag (or 1½-plus pounds) of salad greens in the bowl.

2. Add 2 to 3 cups of berries—a combination of fresh blueberries, sliced strawberries, blackberries, and raspberries.

3. Top with ¾ pound or so of crumbled feta cheese.

4. Add 1½ to 2 cups of nuts of any kind. I used glazed cashews.

5. Be prepared with 2 cups of dressing. Start by stirring in half that amount. Add more if needed. I used balsamic vinaigrette. Raspberry vinaigrette would be delicious, too.

You get the idea. It's a versatile plan. You can use different fruits or cheese or nuts or dressing.

SALADS to INSPIRE

Think flavor, color, and texture!

- **A summer salad** starring ripe tomatoes, scallions, red and yellow bell peppers, fresh parsley, lemon zest, and cooked rice, with a dressing of fresh lemon juice, coarsely ground black pepper, and a light oil

- **A main-dish Greek rotini salad** with both black beans and kidney beans, grape or cherry tomatoes, scallions, cucumber slices, black olives, feta cheese, and herbal vinegar blended with oil

- **A tarragon chicken salad** with cubed chicken breast, red and green grapes, fresh snow peas, and a plain yogurt dressing swirled with fresh tarragon and lemon juice, topped with chipped-up cashews

- **An egg and avocado salad** with chunked hard-cooked eggs and avocados brought together with lemon juice, garlic salt, and coarsely ground black pepper, eaten as is or on toast

Fruit Salad Pairings

Here are some fresh fruit suggestions to get your creative juices flowing:

- sliced peaches and blueberries
- grapefruit supremes with sliced plums and thinly sliced honeydew
- watermelon cubes, halved white grapes, and shaved dark chocolate
- strawberries (halved if large), orange supremes, and plain Greek yogurt
- strawberries (halved if large), blackberries, and fresh mint leaves
- blackberries and cubed cantaloupe with a dash of sea salt
- pear and apple slices with hazelnuts, lemon juice, and maple syrup
- grapefruit and orange supremes, thinly sliced plums, coarsely ground black pepper, and simple syrup
- sliced peaches, sliced beefsteak tomatoes, and broken feta cheese

Using Acids to Draw Out Sweetness

I have a tendency to seek fruits that are ripe, or I wait until they're ripe to use them. But my parents and friends who have emigrated from warm-climate countries remind me that there is a good way to eat *unripened* fruit.

For example, in Thai and Malaysian cooking, mango or papaya salads are made with unripened fruit. They're served with acids, such as juiced lemons or limes, along with salt and chiles, which act together to bring forth the sweetness of the fruit. Onions and crushed nuts add savoriness and crunch, which also highlight the sweetness of the otherwise starchy, sour fruit.

I love to slice unripened mangoes and liberally squeeze the juice of a lime over the pieces. I finish with a sprinkle of salt and ground red chiles. The combination is delightful. A Mexican friend of mine showed me how to use this same technique with raw jicama, and it was delicious!

We often expect to add sweetener if it's not naturally present in fruit to create umami—that multidimensional taste sensation that becomes a peak experience in flavor combining. But rather than adding sweetness, we can use acids to draw out that sweetness. It's an orchestration of ingredients that are quite different but oddly complementary—somewhat like purple and orange on a color wheel.

Take the edge off the acidic bite in a vinaigrette by mixing in some honey or pomegranate syrup.

FREESTYLE VINAIGRETTES

INGREDIENTS THAT WORK WELL

OIL

Use neutral-tasting oil.
- canola oil
- grapeseed oil

MILD ACIDS

- apple cider vinegar
- balsamic vinegar
- lemon juice
- lime juice

STRONG ACID

- red wine vinegar

SEASONINGS

- fish sauce
- garlic (minced)
- herbs: chopped or roughly torn fresh herbs or dried herbs (see the pairing suggestions at right)
- hoisin sauce
- miso
- mustard
- onion (minced)
- pesto
- salt and freshly ground black pepper
- shallot (minced)
- soy sauce
- Worcestershire sauce

Pairing Herbs and Salad Ingredients

- **Basil** with tomatoes, beans, cucumbers, bell peppers, sweet onions, pesto
- **Chives** with cauliflower, broccoli, carrots, egg salad, tuna salad
- **Cilantro** with potatoes, carrots, hot peppers, pesto, salsa
- **Dill** with tomatoes, bell peppers, onions, green beans, radishes, potato salad, egg salad
- **Mint** with chickpeas, cucumbers, peas, green beans, seafood salad
- **Rosemary** with beans, chickpeas, potatoes, carrots, zucchini, eggplant
- **Tarragon** with tomatoes, peas, broccoli, cauliflower, carrots, tuna salad, chicken salad
- **Thyme** with tomatoes, beans, onions, mushrooms, chicken salad, tuna salad, pesto

USE CITRUS MORE AS A *FLAVOR* and vinegar more as a flavor *enhancer*, like adding salt. If you're putting lemon or lime juice into a dish, add the zest of the fruit as well, whether you're making a salad, a dessert, or something savory. Fresh orange juice isn't a very strong flavor, but orange zest is. You can keep orange zest in the freezer in a small jar and add it when you need a little more citrus punch. —MARGARET

KEEP GOOD-QUALITY, BASIC INGREDIENTS ON HAND to draw from. Instead of having just a bottle of Italian dressing in the fridge, have lemons, fresh garlic, and olive oil, too. While the Italian dressing will work fine in some recipes, it's limiting in others. You can always use the basic dressing building blocks in a variety of ways and balance them however you like. —CHUCK

How to Wing It

Mix the oil and acid in a jar with a tight-fitting lid, shaking it hard until the vinaigrette becomes smooth or emulsifies. Or mix the oil and acid in a blender or food processor.

Taste. If you want, add salt and pepper to liven it up. Taste again and adjust as needed.

Add a touch of mustard or miso, if desired, to deepen the flavor. Taste and adjust.

Dip a mildly flavored vegetable from the salad you're making into the dressing. Taste it. If the dressing works, stop fiddling and dress the finished salad.

Add a bit of minced garlic or onion if the vinaigrette needs more flavor. Or add just a splash of another acid, or Worcestershire or soy sauce. Taste again with a salad ingredient.

Add chopped or torn fresh herbs or a few pinches of dried herbs to the vinaigrette, if needed. Or mix the herbs into the salad instead of the dressing.

Stir the dressing into the salad just before serving.

Store leftover dressing in a jar with a tight-fitting lid in the fridge. Shake it well before using.

Try pouring approximate amounts of vinegar and oil directly into a pint jar. Four tablespoons is the same as ¼ cup, so based on that, eyeball 1, or 2, or 4 tablespoons. If you add more vinegar than you need, you can balance it with more oil.

MAKING VINAIGRETTE

- **Discover the ratio of oil to acid that you like best.** The traditional ratio for a vinaigrette is 3 parts oil to 1 part acid, or 3 tablespoons oil mixed with 1 tablespoon vinegar. Start with that, then taste the mixture. If it's milder than you like, try a stronger vinegar or change the ratio to 1 part oil to 1 part acid. The flavor of the vinaigrette depends on the strength of the acid you use. Think about how it will work with the salad ingredients that you'll put it on.

- **Most vinegars are more acidic than lemon or lime juices,** so experiment with a variety of acids to see which you like best.

- **Keep testing different acids and ratios.** You may find that you prefer one formula or acid with certain salad ingredients and another formula or acid with other salads.

- **You can substitute most vinegars for each other.** The one exception, at least for my taste, is balsamic vinegar, which is fairly dominant. —EVONNE

- **Apple cider vinegar works really well in potato salad.** Toss the warm potatoes in vinegar to give them flavor before adding the mayo. —EUGENE

- **Honey-mustard dressing is just honey and mustard mixed together** until you get the taste you like. You can add some oil and vinegar, too, to thin it out a bit. —MARGARET

ASIAN PEANUT SAUCE

1. **Blend peanut butter** with sesame oil. Start with a proportion of 75 percent peanut butter and 25 percent oil because the flavor comes from the peanut butter.

2. **Thin the mixture** with only a bit of water just so it's pourable. Taste and adjust as needed.

3. **Add some rice vinegar**—barely enough to see—to brighten, and mix. Taste and adjust.

4. **Add some soy sauce**—again, barely enough to see, at least as a start—for a salty, earthy punch. Taste again and adjust.

CITRUS DRESSING

1. **Start with a base** of orange juice (⅔ cup), olive oil (¼ cup), and honey (2 to 3 tablespoons). Taste. Add more of whatever is needed.

2. **Mix in chopped fresh mint,** parsley, and chives (about ¼ cup total).

3. **Add a few chopped raisins** and dried cranberries (2 to 3 tablespoons total). Taste and adjust the flavorings. Consider adding a bit of salt and freshly ground pepper.

MUSTARDY VINAIGRETTE

1. **Blend ¼ cup Dijon or yellow mustard** with 2 to 4 tablespoons chopped, lightly packed fresh herbs—basil, tarragon, or dill, for example.

2. **Add some minced garlic** or garlic powder, chopped chives, and cayenne pepper (start small with ¼ teaspoon and add more in tiny amounts if you want more kick).

3. **Stir in some honey** or maple syrup (½ to 1 teaspoon) to balance the flavors. Taste and adjust.

4. **Add a splash of vinegar** (½ teaspoon) and a nearly equal amount of oil. Taste and adjust.

Feeling Your Way into a Salad and Its Dressing

The squirrels are dropping partially ripe Granny Smith apples off my tree these days, nibbling a few bites and then leaving them on the ground. Deploring food waste, I'm toying with what to do with not-quite-ripe apples with a few squirrel bites missing. Cutting out the bad spots, saving what I can, and cooking the pieces down for applesauce would work. But I'm in the mood for something more summery.

So first I squeeze lots of lemon juice into a bowl to keep the diced-up apples from going brown, and then I stir in lemon zest. I'm after as much of the lemon as possible. Orange juice and zest also work well to keep apples from browning, and they add a different flavor than lemon.

My sequence is to put citrus acid into the bowl first because of its preserving qualities, but it also adds flavor. I add the oil later—usually just before serving—after the acid has had a chance to penetrate the other ingredients.

These chopped and dressed apples can be used in a number of ways—for a chicken salad, a fennel salad, a slaw with thinly sliced cabbage along with a bit of red onion and a drizzle of olive oil. Recently I used hazelnut oil, which added a nutty flavor that went well with the green apples.

Citrus also keeps avocado from turning brown in guacamole or in other dishes with fresh avocado. Try grapefruit juice, too! Not only is it a strong citrus acid, its bold flavor goes well with avocado.

FREESTYLE CREAMY DRESSINGS

INGREDIENTS THAT WORK WELL

CREAMY BASE

- crème fraîche
- Greek yogurt (plain)
- mayonnaise
- sour cream

EXTRA-VIRGIN OLIVE OIL

SQUEEZE of FRESH LEMON JUICE

HERBS

Use fresh or dried.
- basil
- chives
- dill
- mint
- tarragon

SEASONINGS

- anchovies (mashed)
- garlic or onion (minced)
- pesto (spoonful or so)
- salt and freshly ground black pepper

HINTS

When making a mayo-based salad in the summertime, try stirring in some lime or lemon juice, or even a light vinegar. That adds depth to the flavor, but you don't taste the juice or vinegar as you would with an oil and vinegar dressing.

If you are vegan, you can use vinegar or lemon juice with silken tofu or cashew cream when you're making a dish that calls for sour cream or yogurt.

A little acid goes a long way, and tasting and adding more if needed is much better than adding a lot at once. —EVONNE

YOU CAN SUB PLAIN GREEK YOGURT FOR MAYO. Put seasonings right into the yogurt or mayo so they are distributed more evenly as you mix up a salad. Depending on the salad ingredients, you may wish to add honey to the yogurt or mayo. —BETH

How to Wing It

Spoon the creamy base into a bowl. Stir it vigorously until it can easily be folded into the salad ingredients.

Add olive oil to thin, if needed.

Think about what additional ingredients might enhance the flavor of the whole salad.

Put just a bit of herbs, if using, in one corner of the creamy base. Taste it. If you like the flavor, add more herbs to the whole bowl.

Put a little of the creamy base in a separate bowl and add just a tad of minced garlic or onion, if desired. Taste it. If you like it, add more to the rest of the creamy base.

Experiment with a squeeze of lemon juice in a bit of the base. Does it enhance the flavor? If so, add more.

Shake some salt and pepper into a little of the dressing. Decide if it enhances the flavor. If it does, add more.

Stir a little mashed anchovy, if you'd like a bit more earthiness, into a spoonful of the dressing. If you like it, good. Add more proportionately.

Stir the dressing into the salad just before serving.

FROM MARGARET

HOMEMADE RANCH DRESSING

1. **Combine plain yogurt** (plus a little mayo, if you like) with plenty of chicken granular bouillon or bouillon cubes.

2. **Add dried herbs to taste,** such as dill, basil, a tiny bit of oregano, and thyme.

3. **Let the dressing sit a bit** to allow the herbs to infuse the cold yogurt.

FROM MARGARET

HOMEMADE THOUSAND ISLAND DRESSING

1. **Strain the red brine** from pimentos (home canned are best!).

2. **Whisk in mayo** until the dressing is the color you want.

3. **Add some spoonfuls** of sweet pickle relish. Taste and adjust the ingredients, if you want.

4. **Add smoked paprika** or a little hot sauce, if desired.

Homemade
Thousand Island
Dressing

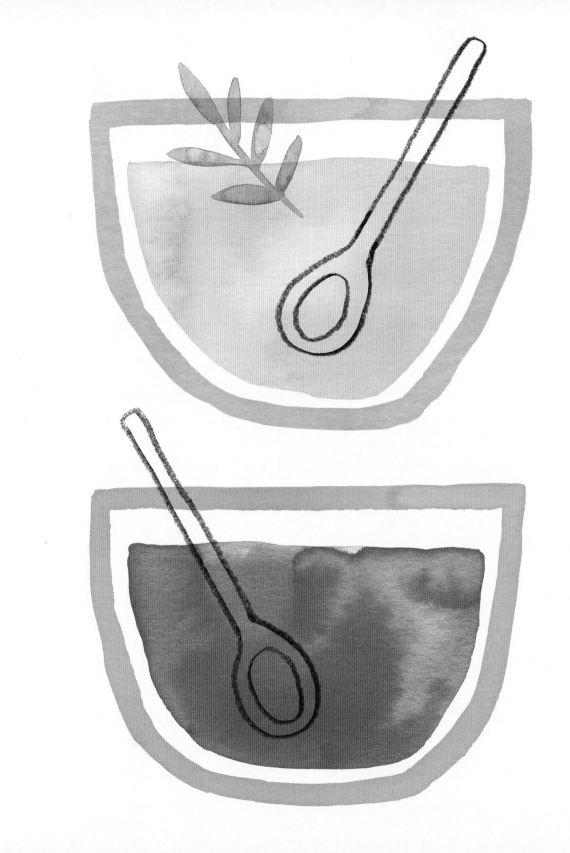

7 / SOUPS

WHEN YOU SET OUT TO MAKE SOUP, don't apologize for making "just soup." Treat it with respect. It's far more than simply fuel or a training camp for cooking without recipes. See if you can make tonight's soup one to cherish. Let it be comforting or exhilarating. Preserve its dignity. Let it call everyone home.

Soup is usually made in logical stages. When the pot is empty, you start by sautéing vegetables or browning meat. Next come the vegetables that need a longer time to cook, along with any grains that take a while and the liquid that will hold it all together. Once the denser vegetables are nearly tender, in go the more delicate vegetables, along with sturdy greens, plus pasta if it's earned its way, followed by seasonings. Taste. Stir. Taste again.

FREESTYLE BEEF, PORK, OR POULTRY STOCK

Tell the waiter you want to take home the bone from the steak or ribs you just ate. Save the wings from the rotisserie chicken you picked up at the store. Hold on to the turkey carcass you have left after carving the holiday bird. Stick bones, sorted by type, into sturdy plastic bags, label the bags, and freeze. Then, one cold winter day, take them out and make stock.

INGREDIENTS THAT WORK WELL

MEAT BONES

- beef bones
- chicken wings or whole carcass
- pork bones
- turkey carcass

VEGETABLES

Seasonal vegetables often don't hold up well under long cooking, or they have too-dominant flavors. Turn to these instead.

- carrot (chunked)
- celery (chopped)
- leeks
- mushrooms
- onions (cut into wedges)
- tomatoes (for added flavor)

HERBS

- bay leaves
- parsley
- peppercorns
- thyme

DEGLAZING LIQUID

- red wine (for beef stock)
- white wine (for pork and poultry stock)

How to Wing It

Thaw the bones if they're frozen.

Preheat the oven to 400°F (200°C).

Spread out the bones on a heavy-duty sheet pan.

Roast the bones for 30 to 45 minutes, or until they're bronzed and brittle.

Transfer the roasted bones to a large stockpot and cover them with cold water. Set the sheet pan aside, but do not wash it.

Add several onions, cut into wedges; a handful of carrots, chunked; and some chopped celery to the stockpot. Stir in parsley, a few bay leaves, some thyme sprigs, and some peppercorns.

Cover the pot and bring its contents to a gentle simmer. Let simmer, unattended, for at least 6 hours and as long as 2 days.

Meanwhile, set the sheet pan over two burners on your stovetop, heat it, then pour on a bit of red wine (for beef stock) or white wine (for pork, chicken, and turkey). Use a wooden spoon to work the drippings loose without letting the pan cook dry. Add the drippings to the simmering stock. You've just magnified its flavor!

Strain out the bones, vegetables, and herbs. Use the stock right away or freeze.

BE A BONE ROASTER. Save chicken and ham bones in the freezer until you have enough to make a tasty stock. If you have time, roast the bones to get that sweeter, darker flavor. Then you've got a base for many different soups.

When I have bone broth on hand and lamb meatballs in the freezer, I bring them together to make one of my favorite soups. I add sweet potatoes and baby bok choy as the broth is heating up. The work of building up flavor for a soup like this happens in stages. —GINI

Family-Style Chicken Soup

My chicken noodle soup is beloved by my family when they're sick or when we need a quick meal. My extended family even keeps chicken bones for me, including my aunt, who also saves her Thanksgiving turkey carcass. In turn, I give them quarts of home-canned chicken stock.

My chicken noodle soup starts with this homemade chicken stock, which I make whenever I've accumulated enough chicken bones in the freezer. I put the bones in a big stockpot with carrot or radish tops that I save from bunches I've bought earlier at the farmers' market—I just wash and freeze them. I use them instead of the parsley or celery that's typically included in chicken stock.

I add a few whole onions—the yellow outer skin is nice for coloring the stock—plus a splash of vinegar and a few peppercorns. I don't risk adding salt at this point because I don't want the stock to be oversalted. (As the stock cooks down, not only does the stock's flavor become concentrated, but so would the saltiness.) When the stock has simmered for a couple of days, I strain out the vegetables and can the broth with my pressure canner.

When I want to make chicken noodle soup, I pour a quart of canned stock into a stockpot. I add a teaspoon or so of dried poultry herbs to enhance the chicken flavor, some salt, lots of freshly ground black pepper, several minced garlic cloves, sometimes frozen corn, and now and then parsley.

Once the stock is boiling, I drop in handfuls of dried egg noodles and continue cooking until they're *barely* al dente—usually several minutes less than the package directions. I cannot bear soggy noodles.

Now's the time to salt the soup. Go sparingly, tasting the stock after you've added the first amount. You can always add more. Sometimes we stir in hot sauce at the table, inspired by Vietnamese chicken soup. Very occasionally, I make a slurry of milk and cornstarch to thicken the soup a little, but not often because it's chock-full of noodles.

This soup is so easy to make that my kids can do it, and so nourishing and satisfying that they want it often. It's quite basic, yet it's deeply loved. I usually serve bread with soup, but not with this because of the noodles. All we need is a veg or fruit of some kind, and the meal is complete.

FREESTYLE VEGETABLE BROTH

INGREDIENTS THAT WORK WELL

CHUNKED VEGETABLES WITH RELATIVELY MILD FLAVORS

Avoid vegetables that are on the edge of spoiling or have distinctive flavors that will tend to dominate the stock, such as cabbage, broccoli, cauliflower, and beets.

- carrots
- celery
- leeks
- mushrooms
- onions
- tomatoes

HERBS

Use those that add subtle flavor but don't stand out.

- bay leaves
- fresh parsley
- fresh thyme
- peppercorns

OLIVE OIL

Use for roasting.

WATER

Use for simmering.

How to Wing It

Preheat the oven to 400°F (200°C).

Mix the chunked vegetables (no need to peel), herbs, and seasonings with oil. Spread on a greased heavy-duty sheet pan with sides.

Roast the vegetables for 30 to 45 minutes, or until the vegetables are tender and bronzed but not burned.

Scoop the roasted vegetables off the pan and into the stockpot.

Add about twice as much water to the pot as there are vegetables.

Simmer the vegetables, uncovered, until the stock is reduced by about half, 45 to 60 minutes.

Strain out the vegetables. Use the stock right away or freeze.

FREESTYLE SOUP FROM SCRATCH

INGREDIENTS THAT WORK WELL

OIL

- extra-virgin olive oil
- vegetable oil

BASE

Use to build flavor into your soup.

- onion (minced; perfect for a classic veggie soup)
- sofrito (chopped onions, carrots, celery, and minced bell pepper and garlic)

MEAT

Include these if you like browned bits in the bottom of the stockpot that can be stirred loose to flavor the whole works.

- beef blade, top round, and sirloin tip roasts
- beef chuck roast
- beef eye of the round steak
- beef short ribs
- chicken legs and thighs, bone-in
- pork butt roast
- pork sausage

CHOPPED VEGETABLES

If it's going to be primarily a veggie soup, add vegetables .

- baby lima beans (fresh or frozen)
- butternut squash
- cabbage
- carrots
- corn
- green beans (fresh or frozen)
- peas
- potatoes (white and sweet)

UNCOOKED LEGUMES, GRAINS, and PASTA

The following are great for texture, and they provide heartiness.

- brown rice
- lentils
- pasta
- pearl barley
- wheat berries

LIQUID

Depending on the liquid(s) you start with, you might also want to add whole milk, cream, or coconut milk as you near the finish.

- broth of your choice
- chopped tomatoes and their juice
- tomato juice
- water
- wine (for deglazing)

CHOPPED GREENS

- collard greens
- kale
- Swiss chard

SEASONINGS

- basil
- chili powder
- cumin (ground)
- curry paste
- hot pepper
- lime juice
- oregano
- paprika (smoked)
- pesto
- salt and freshly ground black pepper
- thyme

If you're aiming for a creamy, milky outcome, any of these are especially good.

- curry powder
- lemon zest
- turmeric (ground)

ACID

Maybe add a splash of:

- ketchup
- lemon juice
- orange juice
- vinegar (apple cider or balsamic)
- wine
- yogurt (plain)

HINT

Use vinegar as a flavor *enhancer*.
Add a small splash of vinegar to the soup at the end just to brighten the flavors— not to taste the vinegar but to perk up the soup. One tablespoon of balsamic vinegar added to lentil soup at the end is perfection. All the flavors in the soup just pop after it's stirred in. —MARGARET

IF YOUR ROASTED RED PEPPER SOUP tends toward the bitter side, balance it with lemon juice rather than vinegar. Sometimes vinegar makes the end flavor of that soup too heavy. —GINI

How to Wing It

Place the oil in the stockpot, heat it, then stir in the base. Or just add oil, and when it's good and hot, stir in bite-size chunks of beef, pork, or chicken, or ground beef or pork, if you're using meat. Brown the meat well, stirring and turning the pieces over occasionally until you have a good fond on the bottom of the pot.

Remove the meat and set it aside. Stir in tomato juice, red wine, or broth to deglaze the pot. Stir vigorously with a wooden spoon over medium heat until you've dislodged all the tasty browned bits on the bottom. Turn off the heat.

Add the chopped vegetables. Think about which ones need to cook longer to soften—potatoes, carrots, green beans, cabbage, butternut squash. Add those sturdy veggies to the pot first, along with dried herbs and seasonings.

Add the cooking liquid. Return any meat to the stockpot if it needs to cook longer to tenderize. Cover and cook over medium heat. Stir now and then to make sure nothing is sticking.

Time your addition of legumes, grains, or pasta so that they and the simmering vegetables will finish at about the same time. If needed, pour in more liquid for cooking the dry ingredients.

Stir in any tender vegetables and chopped greens as the soup nears completion.

Cook until all the vegetables and meat are tender. Stir in any fully cooked meat.

Taste. Does the dish need something more? Consider adding a quick dash of an acid—maybe some ketchup if you have a tomato or tomato-friendly base. Or try lemon juice or apple cider vinegar. How about another splash of wine? Stir in fresh herbs and additional seasonings, taste again, and adjust as needed.

Fill the soup bowls when you've got it right.

SOUP-MAKING TIPS

- **Use whatever good ingredients** you have on hand, especially what's in season.

- **Be ready to double** what you're making so you can feed whoever happens by.

- **Plan ahead** if you're making your own stock. It isn't labor intensive, but it does take hours of unattended time. The flavor of homemade stock is matchless, as will be the soup you make from it.

- **Remember that a splash of acid**—lemon juice, wine, tomatoes, ketchup, vinegar, yogurt—may be the flavor brightener that you're looking for to finish.

- **To experiment with a seasoning,** spoon a little of the soup into a cup. Stir in a smidge of the seasoning. Or add a bit of the seasoning off to the side in the cooking pot. Taste. If it works, you can add more to the whole pot. If it doesn't, you haven't ruined the whole batch.

Butternut Squash
as a Constant

Butternut squash goes in virtually all the soups I make. If I can, I grow enough squash in the garden to last all winter long. Or I buy seven or eight large squash in the fall and keep them in the basement throughout the winter.

I use them little by little, cutting off what I want and storing what remains in the fridge, where it will keep for weeks.

I peel off the rind before adding the squash to the soup. If I want the squash flavor to be noticeable, I cut it into 1-inch cubes. Otherwise, I make ½-inch cubes and mash them against the side of the pot as I stir. If the soup boils long enough, the squash disappears into the broth so that its essence becomes part of the background flavor. It's like the role the third violin plays in a symphony orchestra. You don't really notice that instrument as the orchestra plays, but something is missing if it's not there.

Squash adds a touch of natural sweetness that enhances the other flavors, but without an overtly sweet taste.

When the soup is nearly finished, I usually throw in a handful of chopped greens—say, spinach or kale—not so much for flavor but because we're all supposed to eat more leafy green vegetables, right?

FROM BETH AND LORRE

CHICKEN RICE SOUP

WHOLE GRAINS

such as barley, wheat berries, and brown rice have their own subtle flavor, and they also add a succulent chewiness to soup broth that makes the taste of the liquid so much more interesting in your mouth. That mouthfeel is often more important to me than the precise flavor that the whole grains give. When my family has soup, it's usually the meal entrée, so the heartiness of whole grains gives the soup the stature of a main course.

—DARYL

1. **Chop and mince** onions, celery, garlic, carrots, and bell peppers.

2. **Sauté the vegetables** in oil in a stockpot.

3. **Add chicken broth.** Cover the pot and bring the soup to a boil.

4. **Stir in rice.** Reduce the heat to a simmer and cook until the rice and vegetables are tender, stirring occasionally so nothing sticks.

5. **Stir in cooked chicken.** Heat through.

6. **Season to taste** with salt and pepper.

7. **Finish** with a splash of lemon juice or white wine to brighten the flavor, but not so much that you can taste the lemon or wine. Taste again and adjust to make sure it's as you like it.

8. **Serve** with red pepper flakes.

STORIES FROM THE COOKING CIRCLE: **EUGENE**

Beef Vegetable Soup Base

To paraphrase Mark Twain, the difference between homemade beef vegetable soup and store-bought canned is like the difference between lightning and the lightning bug. My beef vegetable soup varies each time I make it, but the basic ingredients are what gives it the rich flavor.

I start by browning beef. I like to cube a London broil. Because it's important to brown the beef well, I turn each piece with chopsticks. They're great for reaching into a deep pot and picking up individual pieces of meat.

When the browning's done, I add some tomato juice or sometimes V-8 juice and deglaze the pot. Then I pour in the broth and stir until the browned bits dissolve into the liquid.

CARROT SOUP WITH APPLES AND GINGER

ALWAYS KEEP AN EYE on the extra-fresh food you have on hand. "Extra-fresh" is my name for fresh vegetables that should be eaten soon, who are depending on us to include them in a soup or salad before they go past their good lives.

In wintertime, you can put the extra-freshes into a soup, make them part of a stir-fry or pilaf, or stir them into quinoa or pasta. In warmer weather, include them in a salad—green, pasta, or rice. You can make an excellent pasta or rice salad with extra-freshes and creamy dressing. —EVONNE

1. **Chop or slice** lots of carrots and toss into a stockpot.

2. **Chop or slice** apples (enough to both round out and underline the carrot flavor)—peeled or not—and add them to the pot.

3. **Stir in** minced or grated fresh ginger.

4. **Pour in** chicken broth and bring to a boil.

5. **Cover.** Reduce the heat to medium and simmer, stirring up from the bottom occasionally.

6. **Stir in honey,** salt, and pepper when the carrots and apples become falling-apart tender.

7. **Taste.** Add more of whatever flavoring is needed.

8. **Stir in orange juice.** Taste. Balance the flavors, if needed.

9. **Add** a few tablespoons of olive oil.

10. **Purée** with an immersion blender (if you're lucky enough to have one; if you don't, add it right now to your birthday gift list) or in a blender or food processor.

11. **Serve,** topping individual bowls with chopped crystallized ginger, for those who want it.

FROM GINI

SPRING GREEN PEA SOUP

1. **Place a lot of shelled fresh peas** in a stockpot.

2. **Add water.** Cover and simmer until the peas are fork-tender.

3. **Add a tablespoon or so** of olive oil. Purée with an immersion blender, stand blender, or food processor.

4. **Season to taste** with salt and pepper.

5. **Top with crème fraîche**, sour cream, or plain yogurt, if you want.

Seasonal Adaptations

Adapt your basic soup seasonally. I often start with a chicken bone broth in the summertime, then add seasonal veggies like okra, tomatoes, fresh greens, and peas. At other times of the year, I use more root vegetables and sometimes pasta, usually egg noodles.

In winter, I love to make a brothy soup base with pork sausage. For seasoning, I rely on the sausage to start, adding a little more of whatever it has in it to enhance the flavor. Sometimes I go with kielbasa, other times Italian sausage, and sometimes a Cajun blend. I start by browning the sausage in a stockpot, retaining all its drippings. Then I add kale or Swiss chard, apples, onions, sometimes garlic, and finally broth and let it all simmer together. It's a flavorful departure from beef stew that still provides a warm and hearty winter meal. —LINDSEY

BLACK BEAN CHILI

Sometimes I serve this over pasta, topping it with the garnishes.

I LOVE VEGETABLE SOUP OR STEW.
I include garlic, onion, potatoes, green beans, peas, corn, carrots, celery, and Italian seasoning. Sometimes the base is tomato (from a can or two of diced tomatoes), and sometimes the base is vegetable broth. You could add pearl barley to make it heartier. This simple and colorful soup works because it brings together basic vegetables that complement each other. —EVONNE

HINTS FROM DARYL

- **Like Mexican-flavored soup?** Include paprika, oregano, several different kinds of hot peppers, and plenty of red beans.
- **Want a more Middle Eastern feel?** Season with lime, cumin, some coriander, and plenty of lentils.

1. **Sauté minced garlic and onion** in oil in a stockpot over medium heat until soft.

2. **Add cooked black beans,** diced tomatoes, corn, cooked chickpeas, and tomato juice if you're using fresh tomatoes.

3. **Simmer** until the flavors blend. Add salt, pepper, and smoked paprika to taste.

4. **Stir in** some lime juice. Taste again. Adjust the seasoning or acidity as needed.

5. **Ladle the soup** into bowls and serve with whatever garnishes you and the people at the table like.

MISO SOUP WITH CHICKEN BONE BROTH

Sample the globe! Says Zahra, "This combination works well because the soup is salty, slightly sweet, and fermented, and it feels velvety on the tongue." Play with the amounts of each ingredient until you find what you like.

1. **Bring chicken bone broth** to a boil over medium-high heat in a large stockpot.

2. **Stir in kombu** (look in an Asian grocery for this type of kelp). It will add sea saltiness to the stock.

3. **Chop firm tofu** and add it to the stock. Heat for about 10 minutes, or until the soup is warmed through.

4. **Blend in miso paste.**

5. **Serve,** topping each bowl with scallions, seaweed curls, and bonito flakes, if you wish.

TASTE OF INDIA RED LENTIL SOUP

Some folks insist on adding chopped green serrano chiles to this soup. The chiles do make it delicious, yet they add a spicy heat that may not be for everyone. But if you like heat, don't omit this ingredient!

1. **Toast black mustard** and cumin seeds, ground turmeric, and bay leaf in oil in a skillet over medium heat just until you hear the pop of a mustard seed.

2. **Stir in minced or sliced garlic** and fresh ginger. Cook over medium-low heat just until the garlic softens and you can smell the ginger.

3. **Add dried red lentils** and boiling water. The typical ratio is 1 cup lentils to 2 cups water, but play with this if the finished soup is too thick or thin for you.

4. **Add chopped zucchini,** carrots, and chopped chiles, if you want.

5. **Cook the soup** until the lentils bloom into fluffy little rounds and the vegetables are softened.

6. **Taste.** Add salt and a pinch of hing (asafoetida) if you're feeling adventuresome.

7. **Stir in chopped fresh cilantro** and some squeezes of lemon juice just before serving.

HAM AND BEAN SOUP

1. **If you're using dried beans** (any kind you like) and uncooked ham, put the beans, ham, and a good bit of water into a stockpot. Cover and let simmer until the meat is falling off the bone and the beans are tender but not mushy.

    If the beans and the meat are already cooked, heat them up in stock. As you add the liquid, think about how brothy or chunky you want the final soup to be.

2. **Stir in vegetables,** such as onions, carrots, or celery, chopped or sliced, if using.

3. **Cook** until everything's tender and heated through.

4. **Stir in seasonings,** such as thyme, dry mustard, black pepper, smoked paprika, bay leaves, ground nutmeg, or chipotle pepper, if needed. Taste. Does the soup need salt? Anything else? Add and adjust until you're happy.

5. **Serve** immediately if you like the consistency. If you'd prefer it smoother, run an immersion blender through the soup until it's the way you want it.

POTATO AND LEEK SOUP

1. **Decide** whether or not to peel the potatoes. Chunk or cube them. Toss them into a stockpot.

2. **Wash the leeks well,** then chunk or slice them. Use as much of the green parts as you like. Add the leeks to the pot with the potatoes.

3. **Add broth** and cook over medium heat until the potatoes and leeks are tender.

4. **Season to taste** with salt and pepper.

5. **Decide whether to drain off** any cooking liquid.

6. **Eat as is,** or add milk, half-and-half, or cream, if desired.

Backup Meals

I *love* having backup meals in the freezer! This works best for me in cold weather. In hot weather, I depend on fresh vegetables and bread and cheese to make a simple meal. In cold weather, I always try to double a chili or other bean and vegetable soup recipe to have a meal's worth of soup in the freezer. (I don't do this with cream-based or white soups.)

We eat meat sparingly, so if I make more meat or chicken than we will eat at one meal, I put the extras in the freezer (labeled). Then all I need to add is a veg and a carb for a quick meal.

It is important to realize that the fastest meal you have is what's left over in the fridge. A meal in the freezer is also great if you remember to thaw it before you need it!

Thanksgiving Pho

For the last few years, as we're cleaning up from the Thanksgiving feast, I have cut off all the meat from the carcass and immediately thrown the bones in a big pot with water, several onions, large pieces of ginger that I've roasted on the grill and then peeled, and the requisite Vietnamese pho spices (star anise, cinnamon, a bit of lump sugar, and fish sauce). This all simmers as we go about other holiday and family activities.

When it's time for the next meal, or a meal the following day, people always seem delighted to have something different from the standard heavy holiday fare. This also takes care of having to deal with the carcass later after the holidays, when there are plenty of other things to catch up on.

There are other soups in this same vein of a clearish broth with fresh ingredients. One such example is Mexican pozole, where you add chopped cabbage, cilantro, and jalapeño, along with sliced radishes and lime, to a spicy pork or chicken broth.

CLAM CHOWDER NEW ENGLAND-STYLE

Homemade clam chowder has amazing flavor, is fun to make, and offers a fetching combination of textures.

1. **Brown salt pork** or bacon in a stockpot.

2. **Chop onions** and celery, and sauté them in the drippings.

3. **Cube potatoes** (peeled or not). Add them to the pot, along with clam juice and enough water to cover. Cook the potatoes until tender.

4. **Stir in clams** (fresh or canned), butter, and cream.

5. **Season to taste** with thyme, salt, and pepper until you like the flavor balance.

6. **If you want to thicken the chowder,** mix together ½ cup cold water and 2 tablespoons cornstarch in a small bowl until smooth. Add it to the hot broth, stirring continually until it thickens.

BEEF BURGUNDY SOUP *SOBRE*

Leftover beef Burgundy is the base for this rich and thick soup. Simply add vegetables, pasta or barley, and liquid.

1. **Chop or slice** raw vegetables (anything you are hungry for). If you have the time and interest, sauté them in oil in a skillet over medium heat until they're almost tender.

2. **Put the cooked and uncooked vegetables** in a stockpot. Stir in the leftover beef Burgundy.

3. **Decide** whether to add pasta (such as orzo) or barley.

4. **Add stock, broth, or wine** if needed for flavor or to thin the soup.

5. **Cook over medium heat** for 20 to 30 minutes, stirring occasionally, until the vegetables are tender and everything is warmed through.

Soup *Sobre!*

Work with what you already have. Commonly referred to as *leftovers*, your on-hand food is like money in the bank. I like the attitude expressed in the Portuguese word *sobre*, which means both *above* and *beyond*, and is the word Brazilians use to talk about the food in their fridges. Or *planned-overs*, as one of my friends unashamedly names them. —JAY

SPAGHETTI SAUCE AND MARYLAND CRAB SOUP *SOBRE*

Leftover spaghetti sauce is mixed with leftover or fresh vegetables, seasoning, and crabmeat for a delicious meal.

1. **Heat spaghetti sauce** and chicken broth in a stockpot over medium heat until the mixture comes to a simmer.

2. **Stir fresh, frozen, or already-cooked vegetables**, such as finely cubed potatoes, chopped onions, corn kernels, thinly sliced carrots, or small lima beans, into the brothy sauce. Simmer until the vegetables are tender or warmed through.

3. **Season to taste** with Old Bay and chili powder until the flavor is the way you want it.

4. **Stir in claw or lump crabmeat** and continue heating the soup just until the crab is warm.

BEEF AND MACARONI SOUP *SOBRE*

Leftover spaghetti sauce and cooked macaroni are transformed into a beefy, seasoned soup.

1. **Brown ground beef** and chopped garlic together in a stockpot over medium heat.

2. **Add beef broth,** bring to a boil, then stir in either raw or cooked macaroni pasta. Reduce the heat. If you're starting with raw macaroni, cook it a few minutes less than the package directs.

3. **Stir in spaghetti sauce** and ketchup or tomato paste and cook until everything is warm.

4. **Season with herbs**—like oregano, basil, rosemary, and thyme—to taste. Adjust again just before serving.

STORIES FROM THE COOKING CIRCLE: **LINDSEY**

Impromptu Soup *Sobre*

Recently I had some leftover baked chicken and leftover steak that we were planning to eat on two consecutive nights that same week. Then we were invited to an impromptu dinner out with friends, and on another night my son's soccer practice ran very late and we ended up ordering something to pick up while we were still waiting at the soccer field. Now I suddenly had leftover food that really needed to be eaten, and I knew we weren't going to eat it in time.

I chopped up all the meat with some mushrooms and onions and put everything into the slow cooker. I added beef broth from the freezer, along with salt and black pepper, a bay leaf, a few cloves of garlic, and some thyme. I let it cook into a nice brothy stew.

It's summer, and 90°F (32°C) outside. Nobody wants beef stew right now. So when it was finished, I let it cool and froze it. Once the weather cools off and it starts to feel like fall, we'll have a delicious treat on hand!

BEEF or LAMB MUSHROOM SOUP *SOBRE*

This is a great way to get pleasure a second time from cooked steak or lamb.

1. **Sauté chopped onions** and minced garlic in oil in a large stockpot over medium heat.

2. **Add** cubed or sliced cooked beef or lamb, sliced mushrooms, chopped bell pepper, beef broth, red wine, and fresh rosemary.

3. **Heat through,** or cook until the vegetables are as tender as you like them.

4. **Season to taste** with salt, black pepper, and other seasoning.

5. **To thicken the soup,** remove ½ cup of the broth. Put it in a jar and add 2 tablespoons or so of flour. Place the lid on tightly and shake until completely mixed. Alternatively, mix ½ cup cold water and 2 tablespoons cornstarch in a jar. Stir into the bubbling soup until it thickens.

WORKING WITH LEFTOVERS

Margaret shared these great ideas:

- **Leftovers need to be handled diplomatically.** Meals are not just calories to fuel our bodies but also presentation, effort, love, and deliciousness. There's no need to apologize for leftovers *ever*, but a clever cook will spiff them up a bit.

- **Leftover vegetables can be puréed** with stock or a white sauce and heated as soup. In fact, puréed soups can hide a lot, sort of like a green smoothie that has vegetables mixed in with the sweet fruit.

- **I've started calling leftovers "food in the fridge"** to rebrand them for my kids especially, who tend to turn up their noses at leftovers.

How Much Seasoning Is Too Much?

When does the flavor of a dish get muddled? Everyone probably has a different answer, but Eugene limits himself to salt and black pepper when he's making beef vegetable soup. He steers away from strongly flavored seasonings, as well as those vegetables with a tendency to dominate. You may disagree with the particular seasonings and vegetables that Eugene omits. But think about how each element you add affects the flavoring of the finished dish.

You might say, "That sounds like a boring soup. Where's the garlic, red pepper flakes, thyme, other seasonings?" The flavor base of beef and tomato is robust but still allows each vegetable to have its unique taste. For me, adding garlic and herbs homogenizes the overall flavor of the soup, imparting its flavor especially to the carrots and potatoes.

Bell peppers and broccoli have the same effect—they have strong flavors that don't coexist well with more subtly flavored vegetables. —EUGENE

CHICKEN WITH LEMON SOUP *SOBRE*

Already cooked chicken just slides right into this delicious broth and medley of vegetables, adding subtle flavor and heartiness with no extra work!

1. **Sauté chopped carrots,** mushrooms, bell pepper, and onions in oil in a large stockpot over medium heat just until tender.

2. **Add chicken broth,** lemon juice, and white wine.

3. **Bring the liquid to a boil** if you'll be adding pasta. Stir in the pasta. (Alternatively, thicken the broth as described in step 5 of Beef or Lamb Mushroom Soup *Sobre* on page 236.)

4. **Stir in** cubed or rough-chopped cooked chicken when the pasta is nearly cooked.

5. **Add salt and black pepper,** but less than you think you'll need. Taste. Consider adding more lemon juice and/or wine to brighten the flavor. Continue tasting until you've got it the way you want it.

8 / SHEET-PAN MEALS

THERE'S NOTHING LIKE A FLAVORFUL, beautiful meal with only one pan to clean up! Plus, sheet pans are an open invitation, ready for your favorite combinations. Think broadly: breakfasts, brunches, and main meals, plus sandwiches, sliced fruit, and cheesy snacks. Figure out what foods will sing together on a baking sheet and what seasoning will make it all harmonious, or at least interesting.

Sheet-pan cooking is pretty simple, but consider these questions before you switch on the oven:

- **Can all the elements** you're considering putting on the sheet pan cook at the same temperature without any casualties?

- **Do all the elements** require about the same amount of time in the oven, especially if they're cubed or cut up? If so, you're well on your way.

- **Will you be nearby** so you can stage things if the elements require different cooking times, putting the longer-cooking food in first, then adding more delicate elements later in the cooking process?

FREESTYLE SHEET-PAN MEALS

INGREDIENTS THAT WORK WELL

BIG PROTEINS

- beef (steak, sliced tenderloin, chunked chuck roast, ground, meatballs, meatloaf)
- chicken (whole roasting chicken, thighs or breasts, bone-in or boneless and skinless)
- fish fillets
- pork (chops, ribs, tenderloin, whole or sliced)
- sausage links (fresh or smoked, sweet or hot, pork or chicken)
- scallops
- shrimp
- turkey (thighs or breasts, cut into serving-size pieces or chunked)

VEGETABLES

- asparagus
- broccoli
- Brussels sprouts
- cabbage (red and green)
- cauliflower
- corn kernels
- eggplant
- garlic
- green beans
- kale
- mushrooms
- onions
- peppers (bell and hot)
- potatoes (white and sweet)
- spinach
- summer squash (all varieties)
- Swiss chard
- tomatoes (fresh and sun-dried)
- winter squash (all varieties)

BEANS

- black beans
- chickpeas
- Great Northern beans
- kidney beans

FRUIT

- apples
- apricots
- bananas
- berries
- cherries
- pears
- pineapple
- plums

EGGS

FAT

- butter
- fruit-flavored oil
- nut butter
- olive oil

CONDIMENTS

- fish sauce
- harissa
- ketchup
- mayo
- miso
- mustard
- pesto
- pomegranate sauce
- salsa
- Sriracha sauce
- tamari

CHEESE

Use all kinds: soft, grated, crumbled, sliced.

ACID

- ketchup
- lemon or lime slices or juice
- tomato sauce or paste
- vinegar
- yogurt

SEASONINGS

- bay leaves
- capers
- caraway, mustard, fennel, and coriander seeds
- chives
- cilantro
- cumin
- curry powder
- dill
- honey and maple syrup
- paprika (smoked or sweet)
- parsley
- pickles
- red pepper flakes
- rosemary
- sage
- salt and freshly ground black pepper
- tarragon
- thyme

BREADCRUMBS and PANKO

243

sheet-pan meals

How to Wing It

START BY PAIRING FLAVORS—will they go well together? Look for a contrast in textures— some crispy things, some smooth things. Will there be a pleasing contrast in color on the plates?
—GINI

Butter the sheet pan or cover it with parchment paper. Preheat the oven to between 300°F and 450°F (150°C and 230°C), depending on the ingredients and their quantities.

Set out whatever combination of ingredients you're hungry for. Chunk or chop whatever should be cut smaller to cook evenly.

Toss the ingredients with oil, then spread them out in a single layer on the sheet pan. If all the ingredients will cook at the same temperature and for the same amount of time, put them together. If things will cook for different lengths of time, first oil those things that need to cook the longest and place them on the sheet pan.

Roast until everything is tender, or until you're ready to add those additional (oiled) elements that need just a little cooking. Check occasionally that nothing is overcooking. Remove anything that's on the verge and tent it with foil.

Taste. Adjust, if needed, with seasonings or an acid until you get it the way you want it.

244
sheet-pan meals

TIPS FOR MAKING SHEET-PAN MEALS

- **Keep ingredients in a single layer** as much as possible. Direct contact with the baking sheet creates browning and caramelization.

- **For easy cleanup,** use a paper towel spread with cooking oil or butter to lightly coat the surface of a sheet pan or baking dish and reach into every corner. It's old school and gets your hands messy. And yes, you'll have a greasy paper towel to discard, so please use biodegradable, compostable paper towels.

- **You can use parchment paper** to line the sheet pan, but search for a kind that is reliably biodegradable and compostable. Many are not because the paper has been treated to be reliably nonstick.

- **Yes, you can use reusable silicone mats.** But know that these often stand between the pan or dish and the crispy, browned finish on the food that you were hoping for.

- **Mix all your ingredients in a big bowl** when stirring in oil or seasonings. Trying to mix on a sheet pan can be tricky— ingredients tend to jump off. With a big bowl, you've wasted no time because you're not fishing stuff off the counter or floor, you've kept your blood pressure in check, and whatever you're cooking has been well coated.

PORK CHOPS AND FRUITY VEGETABLES

1. **Preheat the oven** to 375°F (190°C).

2. **Brush the tops and bottoms** of the pork chops with oil. Sprinkle with salt and pepper.

3. **Place the chops** in the center of a sheet pan.

4. **Toss cubed sweet potatoes** with oil and seasoning, then place along the edges of the pan.

5. **Roast** for about 35 minutes, or until an instant-read meat thermometer registers 135°F (57°C) (the USDA recommends 145°F/63°C) when stuck into the center of the chop (not against a bone) and the potatoes are tender.

6. **Lay sliced apples** over the potatoes.

7. **Drizzle everything** with maple syrup.

8. **Broil** for a minute or two, just until the apples wilt and the chops brown.

SAUSAGE LINKS WITH WARM AND WILTED GLAZED CABBAGE AND PEARS

1. **Preheat the oven** to 425°F (220°C).

2. **Prick the sausage** links. Lay them on a greased sheet pan.

3. **Cut the cabbage** into wedges or chop it.

4. **Spread the cabbage** around the sausage, then season it.

5. **Roast** for 15 to 20 minutes, or until the cabbage is softening and the meat is browning.

6. **Flip over** the sausages.

7. **Top the cabbage** with sliced fresh pears.

8. **Place the filled pan** under the broiler for a minute or two, until the pears start to color.

9. **Spoon** threads of warmed preserves (maybe apricot) over the sausage, cabbage, and pears.

CHICKEN THIGHS WITH A GLOBAL SAUCE

1. **Preheat the oven** to 400°F (200°C).

2. **Spread the sheet pan** with a sauce—curry, creamy, enchilada, pesto, fruity—using about half the sauce you have.

3. **Lay on** the chicken thighs.

4. **Place broccoli** or cauliflower florets (or both) and chopped stems around the chicken, making sure the sauce is fully covered so it doesn't burn.

5. **Season** everything.

6. **Spoon** the remaining sauce over the top.

7. **Place the pan on a rack** in the top half of the oven. Roast for 35 to 45 minutes, or until the chicken registers 150°F (66°C) (the USDA recommends 165°F/74°C) on an instant-read meat thermometer.

ROASTED VEGGIE GET-TOGETHER

1. **Preheat the oven** to 400°F (200°C).

2. **Chunk potatoes** (leaving them unpeeled adds color and nutrition) of all colors into a large mixing bowl. Add pieces of carrots, peeled and cubed winter squash, red and white onion wedges, green beans, and grape or cherry tomatoes.

3. **Stir in olive oil** and seasonings, such as smoked paprika, fresh or dried thyme and rosemary, fennel seeds, or mustard seeds.

4. **Spread the vegetables** on a greased sheet pan.

5. **Roast** for 20 to 30 minutes. Stir now and then so everything has a chance to brown without burning.

6. **Squeeze fresh lemon juice** over the top before serving. Taste and add more seasoning if the veggies need it.

FISH AND FRIENDS

1. **Preheat the oven** to 425°F (220°C).

2. **Slice unpeeled potatoes** and red onions. Toss the vegetables in olive oil, salt, and pepper in a large bowl until well coated.

3. **Spread the potatoes** and onions over a greased sheet pan.

4. **Roast** for about 35 minutes, or until the potatoes are almost tender.

5. **Cut Brussels sprouts** in halves or quarters, depending on their size. Break off fresh broccoli florets and cut the peeled stems into small chunks. Toss both in olive oil and seasonings in the large bowl.

6. **Scatter the Brussels sprouts** and broccoli over the partially baked potatoes and onions.

7. **Return the pan** to the oven and bake for another 15 minutes or so.

8. **Top the vegetables** with fish fillets, ideally at least ¾ inch thick. Brush the fish with oil, then season. Scatter lemon slices over the vegetables.

9. **Return the pan** to the oven. Bake for 8 to 10 minutes longer, or just until the fish turns flaky.

STEAK HOUSE

1. **Cut a large onion** (red or white) into ½-inch-thick slices. Combine with just enough oil to coat them well in a large bowl.

2. **Spread the onions** over a greased sheet pan. Season with salt and pepper.

3. **Broil the onions** for about 2 minutes on each side, until they start to soften.

4. **Slice a lot of mushrooms** into ½-inch-thick pieces. Stir the mushrooms into the onions and broil for 3 to 4 minutes.

5. **Brush a very tender steak** (1 to 1½ inches thick) on its top and bottom with melted butter or oil.

6. **Push the onions** and mushrooms onto half of the pan. Place the steak on top of the onions and mushrooms.

7. **Toss asparagus spears** (whole or cut) with oil in the large bowl. Add the asparagus to the pan in a single layer on the open half.

8. **Broil** for 3 minutes. If the onions and mushrooms are as tender and browned as you like, remove them now. Flip the steak and asparagus.

9. **Broil** for another 3 minutes for a rare or medium steak. For a rare steak, remove the meat from the oven and tent with foil. For a medium steak, after broiling, lower the oven rack so it's 10 inches below the broiler. Turn off the broiler and oven and keep the steak in the oven for 2 to 3 minutes.

10. **Remove the meat from the oven,** tent it with foil, and allow it to rest for 5 to 7 minutes before slicing and serving. Top with fresh herbs.

You can stack things. The sheet pan hosts the bottom layer. Place a baking rack on the sheet pan to hold the second layer. Then flavorful things can happen, like what's on top dripping down onto what's underneath. Or add the baking rack and its freight later if it doesn't need to cook as long.

BURGERS AND FRIES

1. **Preheat the oven** to 425°F (220°C).

2. **Cut a raft of potatoes** into fries. Toss with oil in a large bowl.

3. **Spread the potatoes** over a greased sheet pan, one layer thick.

4. **Bake** for 20 to 25 minutes.

5. **Set a baking rack** on the pan over the potatoes.

6. **Create burger-sized mounds** of 80% lean ground beef. (For juicy burgers, don't squeeze or mix them with anything.) Salt and pepper the burgers generously on both sides.

7. **Place the burgers** on the baking rack, allowing at least 1 inch of space around each one. (See the tip on page 256 about how to control the amount of drippings that fall on the potatoes.)

8. **Broil the burgers** and potatoes about 4 inches below the heat source for 2 to 3 minutes.

9. **Flip the burgers** and broil for 1 to 2 minutes longer, depending on how well-done you like them.

10. **Serve** the drippings-covered potatoes and burgers with your favorite condiments.

BAKIN' BACON

TIP: If you don't want the carrots to get hit with all the bacon drippings, cover the baking rack with a piece of aluminum foil. Poke a bunch of holes evenly across the foil with a fork so you've controlled the amount of drippings that can get through.

1. **Preheat the oven** to 375°F (190°C).

2. **Julienne a bunch of carrots** into a big bowl. Mix with oil.

3. **Move the carrots** onto a greased sheet pan. Drizzle with honey.

4. **Set a baking rack** on the pan, over the bed of carrots. Lay thick bacon slices across the rack so they don't fall through.

5. **Bake the carrots** and bacon for about 15 minutes.

6. **Remove the rack** with the bacon. Scatter fresh apple slices over the carrots. Stir in as well as possible. If the bacon isn't crispy yet, put the rack and the bacon back onto the pan.

7. **Bake** for another 10 minutes or so.

8. **Break up the crispy bacon** when the carrots and apples are tender. Mix the vegetables, fruit, bacon, and bacon drippings together. Season to taste.

ROASTED BEETS WITH ORANGES AND CRANBERRIES

1. **Preheat the oven** to 425°F (220°C).

2. **Wash, stem, and peel** fresh beets (of all colors, if you have them). Cut into chunks and place in a large bowl. Stir in oil, salt, and pepper.

3. **Place the beets** on a greased sheet pan in one layer.

4. **Roast the beets** for 20 to 30 minutes, stirring now and then, until the beets are tender but not mushy.

5. **Let the beets cool.**

6. **Peel** a bunch of oranges. Stir the segments into the beets.

7. **Stir in dried cranberries,** more oil (olive or a fruity variety), and some brown sugar.

8. **Serve** with plain Greek yogurt.

9. **To make it a full meal,** lay good bread slices on the pan and top them with whatever cheeses you have around. Broil just until bubbly. Serve with the beets and oranges.

FILLED SQUASH BOWLS

1. **Preheat the oven** to 375°F (190°C).

2. **Cut a winter squash** (or several) in half lengthwise. (Acorn squash works well.) Scoop out the seeds and fibers. Brush oil over the cut sides of the squash, and salt and pepper them. Place them cut-side up on a greased sheet pan.

3. **Roast the squash** for about 35 minutes, or until it begins to soften.

4. **Crumble ground pork** or beef into a big bowl. Season.

5. **Stir in chunked fresh apples** and just enough brown sugar for a hint of sweetness.

6. **Spoon the meat-fruit mixture** into the squash halves.

7. **Roast the filled squash halves** for 25 to 35 minutes, or until the meat browns and the apples are tender.

8. **Serve the squash** topped with leafy greens with a fruity vinaigrette. Crumble feta cheese or tear fresh mozzarella over the top.

EGGS IN A GREEN NEST

1. **Preheat the oven** to 375°F (190°C).

2. **Crumble your favorite sausage** (squeezed out of its casings) or ground beef over a greased sheet pan.

3. **Roast the meat,** stirring now and then to break it up, for 4 to 5 minutes, depending on the quantity, or until it's no longer pink. Remove with a slotted spoon and set aside.

4. **Mix a bunch of sturdy raw greens** (Swiss chard, kale, and spinach work well) with plenty of seasonings but just a bit of olive oil in a large bowl. Make a bed of greens in the pan drippings.

5. **Make evenly spaced depressions** in the greens using the back of a spoon. Slide a raw egg into each depression. Season the eggs.

6. **Spoon the meat** around the eggs. Top everything with grated cheese.

7. **Bake** for 10 to 15 minutes, just until the egg whites are set but the yolks are still runny.

SHEET-PANNED CHEESE SANDWICHES

This is a fun party dish.

1. **Preheat the oven** to 450°F (230°C) if you're going to bake the sandwiches (baking takes longer than broiling but doesn't risk burned bread and undercooked filling), or preheat the broiler. Grease a sheet pan well.

2. **Spread one side** of the bottom bread slices with mayo and place them mayo-side down on the pan.

3. **Spread one side** of the top bread slices with mayo and set them aside until you need them.

4. **Spread the top side** of the bottom bread slices with mustard, apple butter, pesto, or chutney (or nothing).

5. **Top the bread** with multiple slices of cheese, or pile up ¾ to 1 inch of grated cheese.

6. **Lay on savory or sweet things,** too, if you want—sliced tomatoes or mushrooms, lightly cooked asparagus or onions, sliced fresh apples or pears, dried fruit or berries.

7. **Put on the top slice of bread,** mayo-side facing out. If you want, spread the inside of that slice with a flavorful spread that complements the whole sandwich.

8. **Bake or broil** the sandwiches. If you're baking, place the pan in the bottom half of the oven and bake the sandwiches for 6 to 8 minutes per side, or less depending on how quickly the bread browns. If you're broiling, broil for 2 to 3 minutes per side.

Hints for Sandwich Parties

- To customize the sandwiches, invite people to each make their own combination. Participants just have to remember which sandwich is theirs.

- To reduce mayhem, designate one person to be the sandwich flipper for the whole works.

ROASTED APPLES OR PEARS

1. **Preheat the oven** to 350°F (180°C). Grease a sheet pan.

2. **Cut apples or pears**—or both—in half and core them. Place cut-side up on the pan.

3. **Make a granola filling** with such ingredients as oats, brown sugar, butter or oil, chopped nuts, flaked coconut, berries, ground cardamom, ground cinnamon, and/or ground nutmeg.

4. **Generously fill up** the open center of each piece of fruit, letting the mixture spill over onto the pan.

5. **Bake the fruit** for 35 to 45 minutes, or until it's as tender as you like.

6. **Serve with yogurt,** whipped cream, or ice cream.

SWEET PLUMS

1. **Preheat the oven** to 425°F (220°C). Grease a sheet pan.

2. **Cut the plums** into wedges and remove the pits. Spread the wedges over the pan.

3. **Sprinkle the plums** with sugar, freshly ground black pepper, and maybe some cardamom or chopped crystallized ginger.

4. **Bake** for 20 minutes or so, until the plums are a little shriveled.

5. **Drizzle with honey.** Sprinkle lightly with sea salt.

6. **Serve over cake squares,** alongside yogurt, or on top of cereal.

PEACH FRENCH TOAST

TIP: Pour the egg-milk mixture over the slices carefully, allowing it to soak in as you go. You really don't want the pan to overflow.

1. **Preheat the oven** to 400°F (230°C). Grease a sheet pan.

2. **Cover the pan with thick slices** of good bread. If you're feeling decadent, spread the face-up side of each slice with cream cheese or Nutella.

3. **Prick each slice** several times with a sharp-tined fork.

4. **Place sliced peaches** on top of the bread. Sprinkle with chopped nuts, coconut, or granola, if that sounds good.

5. **Beat together** eggs and milk. Add some peach juice, brown sugar, vanilla extract, maple syrup, and melted butter, if you wish.

6. **Pour the egg-milk mixture** over the bread. Let it soak in for at least 10 minutes—or even overnight (in the fridge, covered), if you're planning ahead.

7. **Bake** for 15 to 25 minutes, until the bread is browned and puffy.

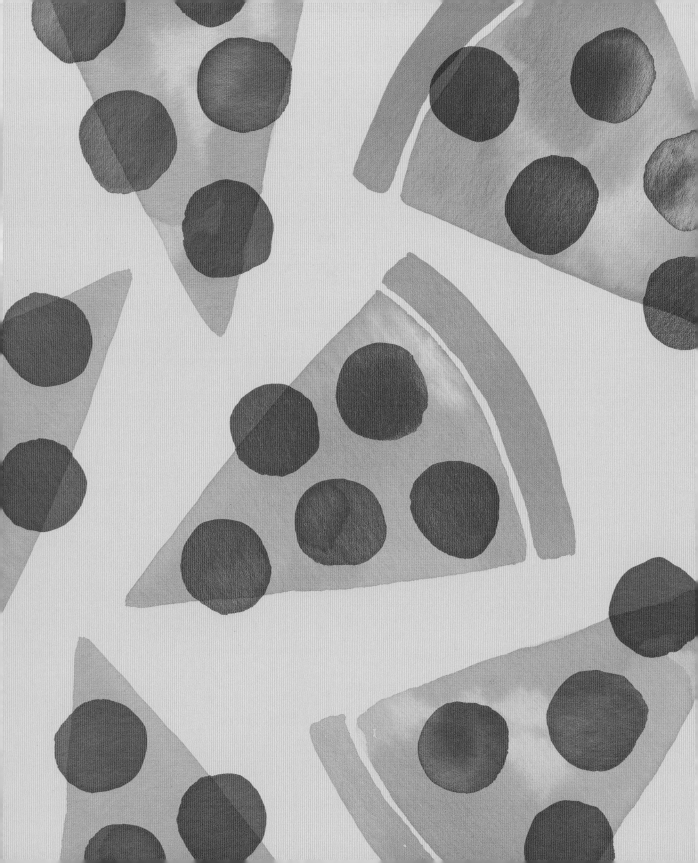

9 / PIZZAS

YOU CAN CUSTOMIZE nearly everything about pizza, making it savory or sweet and including items from clams to pineapple, making it just the way you like it. Search the fridge and the pantry. Bring out everything that's a candidate for toppings, sauces, and cheeses. Then have fun experimenting. These questions will help you get started:

- **What do you especially like about pizza?** The crust? The sauce? The toppings? The cheese? Whatever your answer, focus on getting that the way you want it.

- **What do you want to experience with each bite?** Think carefully about the toppings and don't use too many.

- **What type of crust do you prefer?** Pizza dough is great, but pitas, naan, flatbread, focaccia, and tortillas also work well.

- **Get your sequencing the way you like it best.** Do you want the sauce on first? Or the toppings and then the sauce? Cheese placed against the crust or on top of everything?

- **How did your pizza turn out?** Be alert to whether you want to repeat the pizza you're eating or make changes the next time. It's yours, you know.

FREESTYLE BASIC SAVORY PIZZA

INGREDIENTS THAT WORK WELL

CRUST

- cauliflower puréed in a food processor
- English muffin halves
- flatbread
- French bread halved lengthwise
- naan
- pita
- pizza dough (homemade or store-bought)
- tortilla

EXTRA-VIRGIN OLIVE OIL

SAUCE

- blue cheese or ranch dressing
- fruit butter (depending on what toppings you're using)
- ricotta (spread thin)
- salsa (peach, mango, verde, tomato)
- tomato sauce
- white sauce (see Easy White Sauce, page 268)

VEGETABLES

- asparagus (cut into pieces)
- avocado (sliced, diced, or spread)
- broccoli florets and stems (chopped)
- corn kernels
- edamame
- mushrooms (chopped or sliced)
- red onion (chopped or thinly sliced, raw or caramelized)
- spinach (fresh leaves torn) or Swiss chard (cut into ribbons)
- tomatoes (fresh and chopped or sliced)

BIG PROTEINS

- bacon (browned and broken up or crumbled)
- barbecued chicken (shredded or in small chunks)
- barbecued pork (shredded)
- chipped ham
- clams
- prosciutto (torn)
- roast beef (shredded or sliced)
- smoked salmon
- tiny beef or pork meatballs

CHEESE

Use grated, cubed, crumbled, spread, or sliced, such as:

- Asiago
- Camembert
- cheddar
- feta
- fontina
- Gouda
- mozzarella
- Stilton
- Swiss
- Wensleydale

SEEDS

- caraway
- celery
- dill
- fennel
- sesame

267
pizzas

Easy White Sauce

Stir plain Greek yogurt until it's soft and easily spreadable. Add some finely minced garlic, then stir in chopped chives and fresh basil. Season with salt and black pepper and grate in lemon zest.

How to Wing It

If using a frozen or cold pizza dough ball, bring it to room temperature. Cover it loosely with plastic wrap to keep it from drying out, then let it sit on the counter for 1 to 2 hours. (If you're in a hurry, break one large ball into three smaller balls and bring them together once they've reached room temperature.)

Stretch the pizza dough into the pan or onto the pizza stone. It's more effective to stretch the dough with your fingertips and flat hands than a rolling pin. Gently pull it in opposite directions, turning the dough around and around as you make headway with stretching. Beware of overworking the dough. When that happens, the dough becomes less stretchy because the gluten is toughening.

Prebake the crust at 450°F (230°C) for about 6 minutes, just until it's firm enough to support the sauce and toppings, to avoid a soggy crust. How will you know when you've prebaked it enough? First, poke it to determine if it's starting to set. Then lift up a part of the crust with tongs. If it's still raw in the center, bake until that section sets as well.

Add the sauce, about ½ to 1 cup (depending on the size of the pizza), starting from the center and spreading it out to the edges. Don't drown the crust!

Lightly sauté or microwave fresh vegetable toppings to soften them slightly and to cook off any liquid so extra moisture doesn't soak into the pizza crust.

Spread the vegetables over the sauce.

Sprinkle on the cheeses. Start with the deepest-flavored ones and end with the creamier, milder ones.

Bake at 425°F (220°C) for 10 to 12 minutes, or just until the crust is browning and the cheeses are melting.

Remove the pizza from the oven. Drop fresh herbs over the top and let them soften from the heat of the cheese.

Let stand for 5 to 10 minutes to set up before slicing and serving.

PIZZA-MAKING TIPS

- **A pizza peel or stone** is classic, but if you don't have one, you're not stuck. Use a flat baking sheet, or flip a rimmed baking sheet over and place the crust on the bottom. Without rims, the flat bottom allows air to circulate freely around the baking crust.

- **Keep a few bags of pizza dough** in the freezer. Before leaving the house in the morning, lay a package of the dough in the fridge to thaw. Whoever gets home first can search the cheese and fresh produce drawers for possibilities. Then you can decide whether to add a meat and a sauce.

- **The problem with too many toppings . . .** If you pile them on, you risk having a doughier crust because they can dampen it. Plus the toppings can lose their individual flavors and texture if the mixture is too vast.

GLUTEN-FREE MARGHERITA PIZZA

1. **Rice cauliflower florets** in a food processor, then cook the finely chopped cauliflower until tender. Squeeze the little bits with all your might to remove as much liquid as you can. Then squeeze again— and again. Preheat the oven to 400°F (200°C).

2. **Mix** the nearly dry cauliflower bits with an egg or two, seasonings that mean pizza to you, and grated cheeses that belong with pizza. Bring the mixture together into a ball. Cover your pizza pan with parchment paper. Place the ball of cauliflower dough in the center of the pan and then spread it out across the pan, using a spatula and your fingers. Aim to make the crust ¼ to ½ inch thick, building up the edges a bit more.

3. **Bake for 30 to 35 minutes,** or until the crust sets up and browns. Flip the crust over, using the parchment to manage that. Bake for another 10 to 15 minutes. Remove the crust from the oven but keep the oven on.

4. **Buzz some fresh plum tomatoes** in a food processor until they're saucy. Mix in minced or pressed garlic, salt and freshly ground black pepper, and a tip of olive oil from the bottle. If tomatoes are out of season, pull out that can of San Marzano tomatoes you always have in your pantry (see Ingredients to Have on Hand, page 23). You're after the deepest tomato flavor possible.

5. **Spoon enough sauce** over the crust to just cover it. More, and you risk a soggy crust—but if you don't mind that, go ahead with more.

6. **Top with fresh mozzarella cheese,** cut into small cubes or thin slices.

7. **Bake the pizza** in the oven for 3 to 5 minutes to warm up the sauce and mozzarella.

8. **Top the baked pizza** with grated cheese—mild or sharp—while it's still warm and fresh basil cut into strips.

9. **Cut into wedges** and serve.

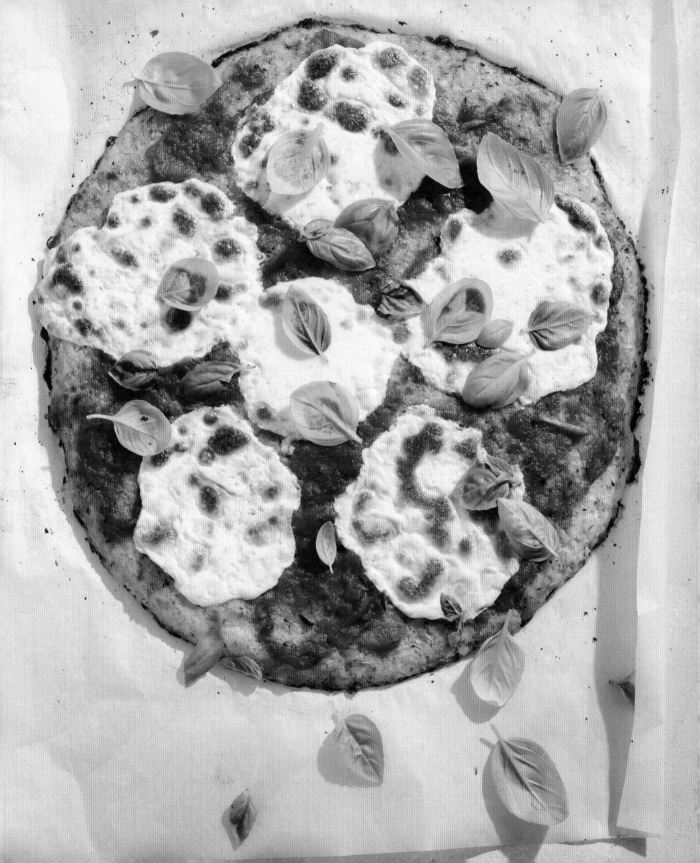

If You're Really in a Hurry . . .

I keep flatbread rounds in the freezer. They make great improv pizzas.

If I'm in a hurry, I stop on my way home from work at our grocery store with a good salad bar and fill up a container with whatever I think would be tasty on a pizza—garlic-roasted kale, grape or cherry tomatoes, sliced onions, olives, feta cheese, Parmesan, peppers, hummus. You'll be surprised at what you can find that's fresh, healthy, and fast.

When I get home, I pull out a flatbread and turn on the oven. By the time it's preheated, I have the pizza ready to go in. I've brushed the flatbread with olive oil, put on the ingredients, and topped it all with cheese. I bake it for 15 minutes or less.

—EUGENE

PIZZA SALAD

1. **Choose your crust.** Bake it so it's ready for sauce and toppings.

2. **Ladle on a sauce** that will anchor or support the flavor of a leafy salad. Maybe it's the salad's dressing, except this time it's under the salad.

3. **Top with a mixture** of leafy greens, along with just-chopped avocado.

4. **Layer on some protein,** if you wish. Try strips of leftover rotisserie chicken, a jammy semihard-cooked egg or two, or a few spoonfuls of edamame or chickpeas.

5. **Add cheese**, perhaps fresh mozzarella slices or chunks.

6. **Add a drizzle** of dressing on top of the greens, if you wish.

7. **Slice** and serve!

AEGEAN PITAS OR FLATBREAD PIZZAS

1. **Toast pocketless pitas** or flatbreads just until they're crispy and lightly browned.

2. **Slather the toasted tops** with hummus.

3. **Layer on** thinly sliced red onions and black olives, along with thin slices of cantaloupe and crumbled feta cheese. If you happen to have prosciutto, or even slivers of thinly sliced cooked ham, lay a few among the feta chunks.

4. **Broil** just until the cheese melts.

5. **Top with torn greens** (arugula is good) and serve.

Pizza Salad

MARKING THE SEASONS PIZZAS

(FOUR VARIATIONS)

Early to Midsummer
GARDEN PESTO

1. **Choose your crust** and prepare it so it's ready for sauce and toppings.

2. **Use pesto** made with just-picked basil leaves as the sauce.

3. **Slice up or roughly chop** what's growing now—red, yellow, orange, and green bell peppers; asparagus; unpeeled eggplants, zucchini, and yellow squash; and mushrooms and onions, thinly sliced.

4. **Layer on the cheese** that seems right, maybe feta, then bake.

5. **Scatter fresh oregano** plus snipped dill and chives, thyme, and/or parsley over the top after baking.

Late Summer
ROASTED VEGGIE

1. **Roast garden tomatoes**—sliced big ones or halved grape or cherry tomatoes. Let the slices char and the grape or cherry tomatoes burst open. Slide them into a mixing bowl.

2. **While the vegetables are roasting,** bake the pizza crust if needed.

3. **Roast thick-sliced onions** along with chunked bell and hot peppers. Add them to the mixing bowl.

4. **Roast thinly sliced cabbage,** along with fresh corn kernels and small chunks of peeled butternut or acorn squash. Scrape them into the mixing bowl.

5. **Put down dollops** of ricotta cheese on the crust, then spread them out to cover the surface.

6. **Spoon the mix** of roasted veggies onto the pizza, draining off most of their juices so the crust doesn't become too damp.

7. **Warm** up everything for 5 to 10 minutes in the oven.

8. **Drop sliced black olives** over the warm pizza top, along with sea salt and maybe some red pepper flakes.

Fall
CHICKEN SALSA

1. **Spread the fully baked crust** with salsa (tomatoey, verde, or herby) that is as hot or mild as you like.

2. **Top** with shredded or cubed roasted chicken.

3. **Place a spoonful** of raw or lightly charred broccoli and/or cauliflower florets over the top, along with sliced caramelized red onions and a handful of edamame. Try a fluttering of finely sliced fresh spinach across the vegetables.

4. **Liberally drop** grated cheese over the top so it will melt lightly across the vegetables.

5. **Slide the pizza** under the broiler for a minute or two so the cheese melts and barely browns the spinach ribbons. Keep watch.

6. **Add extra flavor** after you've pulled the pizza out of the oven by topping it with a handful of pine nuts.

Winter
SAUSAGE AND PEAR

1. **Brush the fully baked crust with olive oil.** Drop on pinches of dried oregano, rosemary, and/or basil, along with some minced garlic.

2. **Cover the crust** with sliced or crumbled hot or sweet sausage. If the meat isn't cooked, bake it on the crust until the meat browns.

3. **Top the meat** with fresh or stewed (and drained) pear and apple slices (no need to peel).

4. **Add a light layer** of crumbled Roquefort or a covering of thinly sliced Swiss or Halloumi cheese.

5. **Broil** for a minute or so, watching closely so the cheese browns or melts but doesn't burn.

Think beyond Pizza Dough

I was introduced to French bread as a pizza crust when I was a kid. We seldom ate out and we never ordered in. My mother was a proper cook who balanced good nutrition, what the garden gave (fresh, canned, or frozen), the meat that my dad chose at the store (he moonlighted as a butcher and knew his meats), and what was reasonably priced.

I learned early on that pizza can take many different forms. We had great family friends who lived on a farm. They would invite us to visit every summer, where they would make what they called Pizza by the Yard. Our host cut a loaf of French bread in half lengthwise. Then she spread it with uncooked ground beef that she mixed with sliced black olives, chopped raw onions, dried oregano, salt, pepper, and tomato paste. She broiled those until the edges of the bread were toasty and the meat topping was starting to char.

But she wasn't done. She had fresh sliced tomatoes standing by and slices of medium cheddar (though you could use whatever cheese you have on hand). She laid the tomatoes over the now-cooked meat, covered them with cheese, and popped it all back under the broiler for about half a minute until the cheese got soft and browned but the tomato slices kept their bright freshness.

I've learned since, when making these for my kids many years later, that there's an important proportion to pay attention to here: the bread should be only about ½ inch thick. If it's thicker, it will turn the pizza experience into a chewing fest where the flavor of the well-seasoned meat is dwarfed by the bread and the fresh tomato mixture sinks into the pillow of the bread and loses its brightness. Get it right, and it's a quick, beloved lunch or dinner, great for an outdoor picnic (or one on the rug).

Also consider other toppings and combinations. For instance, spread the bread with apple butter, then crumble ground sausage or chopped bacon over it. Broil that until the meat sizzles and browns. Then line up fresh pear slices (unpeeled) over the top and push them down into the meat a little. Crumble chunks of blue or Roquefort cheese onto the pears. Slide the works back under the broiler just until the cheese relents and starts to melt. But remember to always keep the bread ½ inch thin.

GREEN-AND-WHITE PIZZA

MY FAMILY paired pitted and halved sweet cherries, sliced red onion, and two kinds of cheeses on a baked crust. We ran it under the broiler after adding the cheese—just long enough to melt the cheese but not soften up the cherries. We loved the combination of sweet and savory!

1. **Choose your crust** and what you're going to bake it on.

2. **Make a white sauce:** Stir together plain Greek yogurt until it's soft and creamy. Add chopped fresh basil, minced fresh garlic, and fresh lemon zest. Taste. Stir in salt and freshly ground black pepper if needed, in small amounts. Depending on the preferences of who's eating, add a pinch of red pepper flakes. Spread a thin layer of sauce over the crust.

3. **Strip a bunch of kale** or Swiss chard of its stems. Pile up a handful of leaves, roll them up, and slice them into ribbons about ¼ inch wide. Strew over the sauce.

4. **Grate fontina** or provolone cheese over the vegetables.

5. **Bake** until the vegetables soften and the cheese melts and browns lightly.

GLUTEN-FREE CHICKEN CUTLET PIZZA

TIP: For an Italian variation, spoon marinara sauce, pepperoni, and fresh mozzarella over the chicken and broil. Finish with fresh basil leaves.

1. **Cut a boneless, skinless chicken breast** or cutlet horizontally so it's no more than ½ inch thick. Now you have your base. Season it with a shake or two of salt and black pepper on both sides. Sauté it in a bit of oil, or broil it, just until it's no longer pink, 1 to 3 minutes per side.

2. **Lay the chicken** on a baking sheet and top with a white or red sauce.

3. **Add a layer** of mild cheese. Stick it under the broiler until it gently melts.

4. **Toss greens** (leafy ones or finely chopped broccoli and/or cauliflower florets) with a couple of squeezes of lemon juice, a few tablespoons of olive oil, salt and black pepper, and some thin slices of Parmesan. Spread the salad across the cheese-topped chicken.

   Or skip the salad and scatter seasoned corn kernels over the chicken. Or add them on top of the salad. Chicken and corn are great partners.

279

FREESTYLE DESSERT PIZZA

INGREDIENTS THAT WORK WELL

CRUST

- chocolate chip cookie dough
- gingersnap dough
- sugar cookie dough

SAUCE

Use individually or in any combination.

- mixture of softened cream cheese, sugar, and lemon juice
- peanut butter
- softened jam or jelly
- whipped topping

TOPPING

- apricots and/or plums (chopped)
- blueberries
- grapes (halved)
- peaches (fresh or canned, cubed or sliced)
- pineapple
- strawberries

GLAZE

- orange juice, lemon juice, sugar or honey, and cornstarch

COOKING OIL

Use for greasing the pan.

How to Wing It

Press the crust into a greased pizza pan.

Bake the crust at 325°F (170°C) for 10 to 20 minutes, or until lightly browned. Cool the crust.

Spoon your choice of sauce over the crust.

Add the toppings you want.

Mix together the orange juice, lemon juice, sugar, and cornstarch in a small saucepan over medium heat. When it's thickened, remove from the heat. Pour the glaze over the fresh fruit to keep it from turning brown.

Chill the pizza for several hours.

Slice and serve.

Pour a glaze
over fresh
fruit to keep
it from turning
brown.

WATERMELON PIZZA

1. **Cut a triangle-shaped slice of watermelon** about 3 to 4 inches wide at the base and 1½ inches thick. This is your pizza "crust" for one serving. Cut more pieces for everyone who's eating.

2. **Brush each slice** with oil on one side, then salt and pepper that same side.

3. **Place the watermelon slices,** oiled-side up, on a baking sheet and slide it under the broiler. Or put the slices oiled-side down into a very hot grill pan.

4. **Broil or grill** for 2 to 3 minutes. Let the watermelon brown lightly, but not cook.

5. **Flip each slice over.** Oil and season the other side. Put that side under the broiler or into the grill pan for 1 to 2 minutes.

6. **Cover each grilled slice** with a small handful of leafy greens.

7. **Top** with fresh blueberries and sliced unpeeled peaches.

8. **Drizzle honey** over the greens and fruit on each slice. Then serve.

LOTSA CHOCOLATE PIZZA

1. **Choose a soft pizza dough** or a cookie dough. Bake it in a pizza pan just until it begins to brown.

2. **Spread a layer** of Nutella all over the lightly baked crust.

3. **Scatter** semisweet or milk chocolate chips, butterscotch chips, or white chocolate chips, or a combination of them, over the pizza.

4. **Top with dollops** of peanut butter and/or a caramel sauce. Add coarsely chopped nuts, broken candy bar pieces, and/or small marshmallows.

5. **Bake** at 450°F (230°C) for 2 to 3 minutes, or until the morsels just begin to melt.

10 / EGGS

ON A BUDGET? SHORT ON TIME? BEGINNER COOK?
Unexpected guests? Eggs have you covered. Eggs are one
of the most commonly available and fastest-to-prepare proteins
around. They are perfect for empty cupboard or fridge emergencies. Always keep them on hand.

Eggs can be prepared in a number of styles (fried, over-easy,
scrambled, soft-boiled, hard-cooked, poached) and added to
an array of dishes. Think of all the ways eggs behave well with
others:

- **Jammy topping** on green salads

- **Sauce** over a bowl

- **Bringer-together** of ingredients in a stir-fry

- **Added protein** when hard-cooked and chunked in a cream
  sauce or salad

- **The base** sitting up proudly in a quiche or frittata

- **Contrasting color and flavor** in a shakshuka

- **Perfect partners** with cheese, vegetables, pesto, and salsa

Sunny-side up

Over-easy

Over-medium

FRIED EGGS

INGREDIENTS

- 1 or more eggs per person
- butter or oil, or a combination of the two
- salt and freshly ground black pepper

STEPS TO TAKE

1. **Break each egg** into a cup (a custard cup if you have one, but a regular cup works, too). Set aside.

2. **Place the butter** in a skillet and heat over medium heat.

3. **Slide the egg** into the skillet when it is hot.

4. **For sunny-side up:** Cover the skillet with a lid. Cook over low heat until the white is set but the yolk is still runny, about 2 to 2½ minutes. Slide the egg onto a plate.

    For over-easy: When the white is nearly set and the yolk is beginning to thicken, flip the egg over. Allow the egg to cook just a few seconds on the second side before sliding it onto a plate.

    For over-medium: Flip as for over-easy, then let the egg cook gently until the white is set and firm and the yolk is thickening but isn't hard. Using a spatula, lift it onto a plate.

5. **Season** with salt and pepper.

THANKING THE GIVER: A chicken gives an egg freely—and some are very proud of what they've done! Cows give milk freely. That's the spirit in which we should treat food—and offer it. —BETH

287

SCRAMBLED EGGS
ON THE STOVETOP

INGREDIENTS

- butter or oil, or a combination of the two
- 1 or more eggs per person
- milk or water
- salt and freshly ground black pepper
- shredded or crumbled cheese (optional)

STEPS TO TAKE

1. **Add the butter** to a skillet. Heat over low heat.

2. **Break the eggs** into a bowl. Add the milk and salt and pepper. Whisk until blended well.

3. **Pour the beaten eggs** into the warm skillet. Use a spatula to pull the eggs that are cooking around the edges into the center of the skillet.

4. **Scatter the cheese**, if using, over the eggs as you continue to pull the cooked eggs into the center of the skillet.

5. **Turn over the eggs** throughout the skillet with the spatula, scooping them up from the bottom when there are no more uncooked eggs running out to the edge of the skillet.

6. **Remove the skillet** from the heat when the eggs are nearly but not quite fully cooked. They'll be shiny and not a bit dry.

7. **Serve** immediately.

SCRAMBLED EGGS ARE VERY USEFUL for incorporating little dabs of leftovers that the family is bypassing for whatever reason. So, too, are fritters. Most food tastes better fried, right? (I don't mess with deep-frying because all that oil intimidates me, and then I have a hard time discarding it all when the frying is done. I just pan-fry.) Mash something up, put an egg and breadcrumbs in it for binding if needed, form it into little patties, and fry away in a hot oiled skillet. My family especially adores cocktail sauce with fritters of any kind: mix equal parts horseradish and ketchup. —MARGARET

SCRAMBLED EGGS IN THE MICROWAVE

INGREDIENTS

- 1–2 eggs per person
- seasonings and herbs (optional)
- salt and freshly ground black pepper

STEPS TO TAKE

1. **Crack the eggs** into a microwaveable cup.

2. **Add seasonings,** herbs if you want, and salt and pepper.

3. **Beat with a fork** until well mixed. Cover the cup tightly.

4. **Cook at 70 percent power** for 45 to 60 seconds, or until the mixture forms clumps but still looks wet. Serve right away.

Cook your eggs too long? Mash them. Chop them fine. Or grate them over buttered toast or a sautéed vegetable.

HARD-COOKED EGGS

INGREDIENTS

- 1 4 eggs

STEPS TO TAKE

1. **Remove the eggs** from the refrigerator and let sit at room temperature while the water heats (they will be less likely to crack if they don't come straight from the fridge when you put them in hot water).

2. **Bring a saucepan** of water to a boil.

3. **Carefully place** the eggs in the boiling water and reduce the heat to a simmer. Keep the pan uncovered and cook for 10 minutes.

4. **Drain** the eggs.

5. **Refrigerate,** or peel and serve. If serving right away, run the eggs under cold water to cool them before peeling.

JAMMY HARD-COOKED EGGS

INGREDIENTS

- 1–4 eggs (ideally 7 to 10 days old)

HINT

- **Monkey around with the timing** if you want the eggs cooked softer or harder next time.

STEPS TO TAKE

1. **Cover the eggs** with cold water in a saucepan.
2. **Cover the pan.** Bring the water to a boil. Boil the eggs for 3 minutes.
3. **Remove the pan** from the heat. Keep covered.
4. **Let stand** for 15 minutes.
5. **Lift the eggs** from the hot water and plunge into cold water.

SOFT-COOKED EGGS

INGREDIENTS

- 1–4 eggs
- salt and freshly ground black pepper
- toast strips for dipping (optional)

HINT

- **Did the egg yolk turn out to be harder than you wanted?** Peel the egg the whole way. Grate the white over a salad or sautéed vegetable, then crumble the yolk over it, too.

STEPS TO TAKE

1. **Lay the eggs** in a saucepan in a single layer. Add enough cold water to cover them by an inch.

2. **Cover the pan.** Bring the water to a boil.

3. **Turn off** the heat. (If you're using an electric stove, take the pan off the burner.)

4. **Keep the pan covered.** Immediately set your timer for 1½ minutes.

5. **Remove the eggs** one by one with a slotted spoon when the timer goes off. Set each one upright in an egg cup or short-sided regular cup. (If they won't stand up straight, pour uncooked rice, lentils, or other uncooked grains around them in the cup.)

6. **Tap firmly but gently** around the top of each egg with a knife so that the shell begins to crack and you can lift off the top.

7. **Season** with salt and pepper, then use a spoon to eat the egg out of the shell. Serve with toast strips for dipping, if desired.

OMELET

INGREDIENTS

- 2–3 eggs per person
- water, half-and-half, or olive oil
- salt and freshly ground black pepper
- extras: vegetables, meat, or cheese (see the list on page 298)
- butter and/or oil (optional)

STEPS TO TAKE

1. **Beat the eggs** in a bowl until well mixed.

2. **Stir in a bit of liquid** so the eggs stay looser while they're cooking. Season with salt and pepper.

3. **Chop or slice** any vegetables or meat you plan to add to the eggs. Grate or crumble any cheese that you'll be mixing in.

4. **Steam, microwave, or sauté** any raw vegetables until they're fork-tender. Drain off their juices as fully as you can.

5. **Add a teaspoon** or so of butter to a skillet (omit if you use a nonstick skillet). Heat over medium heat.

6. **Cook the eggs** over medium heat until the eggs in the center of the skillet have set, about 15 seconds. Lift that center portion of the eggs with a spatula to allow the unset eggs to run into the center to cook.

7. **Spoon extras** over either half the omelet, or over the middle third of the omelet, while the eggs are still wet on top. Use the spatula to fold the empty half of the omelet over the filled half or to fold in each of the empty sides over the filled middle.

8. **Serve** right away.

Fold each cooked side over the middle.

EGG-COOKING TIPS

- **Serve eggs made any way** with pesto, salsa, and/or hot sauce on the side. Offer a bowl of halved grape or cherry tomatoes as an accompaniment, too. Let individuals customize their own plates so everyone's happy.

- **Wish your eggs had more flavor?** Add herbs and/or seasonings.

- **Some fresh vegetables** give off a lot of liquid as they cook—fresh tomatoes and spinach, for instance. When you mix those uncooked vegetables into raw eggs to make a quiche, they can water down the eggs as they heat up. But don't give up on that great mix of flavors. Just bake the eggs fully, then top them with fresh sliced tomatoes or fresh steamed spinach, or serve the fresh vegetables as a side.

- **A lot of extras that are added to eggs**—peppers, onions, herbs, many cheeses, and meats—have strong flavors. Think about what combination of tastes you're after and how much of each extra to add before stirring fistfuls into the cooking eggs.

Extras That Work Well with Eggs

Check the fridge to see what you could chop and add. These "extras" might be fresh or might be leftovers.

VEGETABLES AND FRUITS

- apples or pear slices (peeled or not; especially good with sausage, ham, and bacon alongside the eggs)
- asparagus (cut into pieces)
- beans (cooked; drained if canned)
- black olives (sliced)
- broccoli (chopped)
- garlic (minced)
- mushrooms (sliced)
- onions (chopped; raw or caramelized)
- peas (frozen)
- peppers (bell or hot; chopped; raw or roasted)
- sun-dried tomatoes (slivered)
- tomatoes (fresh and coarsely chopped)

HERBS (FRESH OR DRIED)

- basil
- chives
- cilantro
- dill
- parsley
- rosemary
- sage
- tarragon

MEAT (COOKED AND CHOPPED)

- bacon
- chicken
- ground beef
- ground pork
- ham
- sausage

SEAFOOD

- salmon or scallops (cooked and chopped)
- smoked fish (chopped or shredded)

CHEESE (CRUMBLED OR SHREDDED)

- cheddar
- feta
- fontina
- Parmesan
- Swiss

Don't Stop Yet—Make a Sandwich, Quesadilla, or Burrito!

Spread the insides of a bun, pita, croissant, or slices of toast with mustard or mayo (spicy or not). Spoon in the cooked eggs and extras and serve.

Put a tortilla in a skillet, layer some cooked eggs and extras over it, top with more cheese, then stack on another tortilla to wind up with a quesadilla. Now you have a full meal.

Fold the eggs and extras inside a burrito. Offer chiles, cooked black beans, and chorizo as toppings. This is a very full meal!

BASIC FRITTATA

INGREDIENTS

- olive oil and/or butter
- extras: vegetables and cheese (see the list on page 298)
- 1–2 eggs per person
- half-and-half or milk
- salt and pepper, garlic powder, dill, and/or smoked paprika, if you wish
- buttered toast and applesauce, for serving (optional)

IF YOU HAVE MEAT, VEGGIE, AND/OR POTATO LEFTOVERS, stir eggs, a little milk, and grated cheese into them, along with Italian seasoning, onion, and garlic, and you'll have a frittata. Turn it all into a well-greased ovenproof skillet. If you have several slices of older bread, tear them into breadcrumbs and scatter them over the filled skillet. Bake in a preheated 350°F (180°C) oven for 20 to 30 minutes, or until the frittata is heated through.
—EVONNE

STEPS TO TAKE

1. **Preheat the oven** to 350°F (180°C) if you'll be baking the frittata.

2. **Heat the oil** in a skillet set over medium heat. When it's hot, stir in the vegetables you want to mix with the eggs. Sauté just until soft.

3. **Whisk together** the eggs, half-and-half, seasonings, and half of any cheese you plan to use in a large bowl.

4. **Pour the egg mixture** over the sautéed vegetables in the skillet. Alternatively, if you'll be baking the frittata in a pie plate or ramekins, spoon the sautéed vegetables into the pans. Then pour the egg mixture over the top.

5. **If you're using a skillet** on a stovetop, cook the eggs over medium heat. Occasionally lift the edges of the eggs with a spatula so the uncooked eggs can run onto the bottom of the skillet to cook. When the eggs are just set but still wet on top, turn off the heat.
   If you're using a pie plate, bake for 30 to 40 minutes, or until just firm in the middle. For ramekins, bake for 20 to 30 minutes, or until just firm.

6. **Preheat** the broiler.

7. **Top the frittata** with the remaining cheese and broil just until lightly browned.

8. **Let stand** for 5 minutes before cutting to serve. Serve with buttered toast and applesauce, if desired.

Frittata vs. Quiche

What's the difference between a frittata and a quiche? In general, frittatas are mostly eggs with just a touch of dairy. They include extras, but they don't have a crust. Quiches are usually 1 part egg to 2 parts dairy with extras added, plus a crust. Because a quiche's "custard" part involves balanced amounts of dairy, eggs, and flour, it's best to lean on a reliable recipe rather than improvise the mixture—unless you're experienced or enjoy such experiments.

POACHING

INGREDIENTS

- 2–4 cold eggs

STEPS TO TAKE

1. **Pour 2 to 3 inches of cold water** into a saucepan. Heat until the water boils.

2. **Reduce the heat** so the water is no longer boiling but simmers continually.

3. **Break one egg** into a shallow bowl, custard cup, or ramekin. Don't break the yolk.

4. **Bring the bowl** close to the surface of the simmering water and slip the egg into the water.

5. **Repeat** steps 3 and 4 for each egg.

6. **Cook the eggs,** uncovered, until the whites are completely set and the yolks are thickening but not hard, about 4 minutes. *Don't stir.*

7. **Lift out the eggs,** one at a time, using a slotted spoon. Drain off any water. Let the egg stand in the spoon or place it carefully on paper towels until needed.

Add Poached Eggs To:

- Cooked asparagus spears
- A leafy green salad
- A pizza
- A burger
- Individual servings of a vegetable soup that welcomes a protein
- A bowl, where an egg can bring everything together and even sub for a sauce

303
eggs

A Sweet Potato Bed for Eggs

A cousin was traveling through and we invited him to stay the night, which meant he'd have breakfast at our house the next morning. I had a sweet potato waiting to be eaten, so I diced it into ½-inch cubes (to cook quickly) and put the cubes in a medium-hot cast-iron skillet with plenty of butter. (Coconut oil would work, too.) I added a touch of water and covered the skillet. The goal here was to start to cook the potatoes before they browned in the oil.

I cut up some scallions and added them to the skillet. Then I cleaned some arugula and stout greens (kale, chard, etc.), trimmed off their woody stems, and chopped the leaves so they weren't too large. With the skillet off the heat, I tossed the greens in with the potatoes and scallions until they wilted.

Next, I made little depressions in the skillet mixture, broke an egg into each, and sprinkled everything with salt and pepper.

I crumbled a bit of cheese over the top (a really sharp aged cheddar is good). That's optional, of course. Then I covered the skillet, put it over low heat, and added a bit of water to make sure things wouldn't dry out or scorch on the bottom while the eggs cooked.

As the food did its final cooking, I made tea and cleaned up. This is the time to make a salad or stir a few fresh herbs into a soup you might have going. Just don't forget to check the eggs. When they're cooked to your preferred level of doneness, serve them with hot sauce on the side. I like the flavor habañero adds.

EGG SALAD

1. **Peel and chop** hard-cooked eggs.

2. **Place the chopped eggs** in a large bowl and fold in mayo. Then decide whether to mix in:

   - Sriracha sauce

   - mustard—Dijon, maybe

   - chopped celery and minced onion

   - fresh dill

   - chopped pickles

   - crispy broken bacon

   - diced avocado

   - salt and freshly ground black pepper

3. **Taste.** Does the egg salad need an acid hit, such as lemon juice, or another seasoning? Adjust as needed.

4. **Spoon onto lettuce leaves**, bread, or toast.

More Ways to Use Eggs

Add a raw egg to:

- **A stir-fry with rice.** You'll bring those cooked vegetables and rice together in a satisfyingly saucy finish as you gently stir it all together.
- **A whole fresh tomato,** hollowed out but with a good, thick wall. Fill with a mixture of breadcrumbs, salt, black pepper, chopped basil, melted butter—and an egg, of course. Bake until the tomato is warmed and soft (but not collapsing), the crumbs are browned, and the egg is somewhere between saucy and firm.
- **A greased ramekin.** Crack an egg into the ramekin, then sprinkle the egg with salt and pepper. Spoon grated or crumbled cheese and chopped chives over the top. Bake until a knife inserted into the center of the egg comes out with some eggy bits clinging to it.

DEVILED EGGS

1. **Cut hard-cooked eggs** in half and flip the yolks into a bowl.

2. **Mash the yolks together** with a fork. Then add your choice of mix-ins:

   - mayo or plain Greek yogurt
   - a few dabs of mustard
   - a spoonful of mashed avocado
   - salt, and perhaps black pepper or paprika, too
   - a little pickle juice
   - finely chopped chives
   - finely diced kimchi, mixed in or lightly dropped on top
   - crumbled blue cheese or bacon

3. **Spoon or pipe** the smooth and creamy filling into the whites.

RED BEET PICKLED EGGS

I grew up on these pickled eggs. There is a standout ingredient: red beet juice. It adds a very subtle flavoring, but it turns the egg whites a gorgeous purple-red. When sliced in half, the pickled eggs are stunning—golden yolks surrounded by a rich pink that becomes a deeper red at the outer edge of the eggs.

1. **Drain the juice** from one (15.5-ounce) can of red beets into a saucepan. Stir in about ¼ cup sugar and ½ cup apple cider vinegar. Bring to a boil. Simmer for a few minutes to allow the flavors to become more concentrated.

2. **Put peeled, whole, hard-cooked eggs** into a heatproof container with a tight-fitting lid. Cover with the hot pickled red beet juice. Cover and refrigerate for at least 3 days. The color intensifies with each day.

3. **Lift the eggs** out of the juice, cut them in half, and serve with salt and freshly ground black pepper.

Red Beet
Pickled Eggs and
Mustard Pickled
Eggs (page 312)

MUSTARD PICKLED EGGS

Red Beet Pickled Eggs (page 310) have a cousin. Essentially, you replace the red beet juice with whatever mustard you like the best. Not surprisingly, these taste a little like deviled eggs. Serving these alongside Red Beet Pickled Eggs brings unmatched color to your table.

1. **Combine ½ cup each** of apple cider vinegar and water in a saucepan. Stir in ⅔ cup sugar and a shy ¼ cup mustard. Bring to a boil. Simmer to concentrate the flavors.

2. **Put peeled, whole, hard-cooked eggs** into a heatproof container with a tight-fitting lid. Cover with the hot pickled mustard juice. Cover and refrigerate for at least 3 days. The color intensifies with each day.

3. **Lift the eggs** out of the juice, cut them in half, and serve with salt and freshly ground black pepper.

Painted Eggs

Hard-cook dozens of eggs, then paint them with your family on a weekend afternoon in the spring. My cousin and her tribe of 24-plus extended family members gather to do this every Easter season, and they make it a contest. Everyone votes for the most interesting painted egg!

While we're painting and I'm hiding my sad-looking painted eggs (hey, I'm the kid who lacked a knack for drawing and during art class usually wound up in the nurse's office with a case of the nerves), I'm imagining what memorable egg dish we'll make with all of these hard-cooked eggs in the next few days!

CREAMED EGGS

I first ate creamed eggs when I was on a choir tour in high school. We were in the mountains of West Virginia, and we stayed in a private home after giving our concert. The next morning, as the mists floated past the windows and the peaks of nearby mountains held their heads above the clouds, we gathered around a big table with our host family for a breakfast of creamed eggs.

Serve these to people you love and to guests on whom you'd like to make a memorable impression—whether for breakfast, lunch, or supper.

1. **Peel and chop** hard-cooked eggs. Set them aside.

2. **Make a white sauce** (see page 124).

3. **Stir the chopped eggs** into the sauce.

4. **Serve over** cut-up toast or split biscuits.

11 / TOAST TOPPERS AND THEIR COUSINS

BUY FRESH BREAD AND BREADY COUSINS—flatbreads, focaccia, naan, pitas, tortillas, taco shells—often so you have them ready to go whenever you might need them. Keep at least one pack on standby in the freezer, too. Who knows when the kids will bring the whole team home unannounced? Or a drop-in visitor will stay until mealtime? Or you will work straight up until 5:30 p.m. and come home to a pretty empty fridge?

When you're slicing bread, think about the appropriate thickness. Too thick and the toppings are overshadowed and can't sing. Too thin and the toppings fall together and the bread gets soggy.

These breads are platforms, but with personalities of their own. They aren't pushy, but they play a noticeable part. So choose them for their texture and flavor—and how well they will harmonize with what you'll put on top of or inside them.

FREESTYLE TOAST TOPPERS, FLATBREADS, AND SANDWICHES

INGREDIENTS THAT WORK WELL

BREAD

Select tasty, good-textured bread, flatbread, focaccia, pita, tortilla, taco shell, or naan that is delicious whether fresh or toasted.

SAVORY SPREADS

- butter
- chutneys
- cream cheese
- horseradish
- mustard
- nut butters
- olive oil
- pesto
- ricotta or cottage cheese
- salad dressing
- smashed vegetables, alone (mashed sweet potatoes) or in combination (avocado mashed with chickpeas)
- tahini

SWEET SPREADS

- fruit butters
- honey
- jams
- Nutella

VEGETABLES

Use sliced or chopped, raw, roasted, or sautéed.

- broccoli and cauliflower florets (finely cut)
- mushrooms
- peppers (fresh or roasted)
- pickled onions and cucumbers (thinly sliced)
- tomatoes

FRUIT

Use sliced or chopped, raw, roasted, sautéed, or dried.

- dried plums, cranberries, and cherries
- grapes (halved)
- peach slices (fresh, canned, or dried)
- thin apple slices (peels on or off, fresh or dried)
- thin pear slices (peels on or off, fresh or dried)

SEAFOOD

- cooked shrimp
- crabmeat
- flaked tuna
- smoked salmon
- tuna salad

MEAT

Try the following cooked and sliced, chipped, or shredded, alone or in combination (chicken breasts topped with crispy bacon).

- beef
- chicken
- ham
- pork
- turkey

REINVENTED LEFTOVERS

- beans in a sauce
- browned mushrooms
- caramelized onions

SAVORY TOPPINGS

- adobo sauce
- cheese (to melt)
- fried or hard-cooked egg (chopped or grated)
- herbs (dried or fresh)
- hummus
- lemon or lime juice
- nuts (raw or roasted, broken or chopped)
- olives (chopped)
- pickled vegetables
- salsa
- sun-dried tomatoes

SWEET TOPPINGS

- applesauce or stewed apples
- candied nuts
- drizzles of chocolate, butterscotch, warm blueberry or strawberry, hot fudge, or peanut butter sauces
- melted jams
- shaved chocolate

How to Wing It

Survey the fridge for fresh vegetables or fruits that can be sliced or cut up to sit easily on toast. Think flavor and texture, too, as you select.

Look also for cooked food that can be transformed into a new dish on toast by adding a gravy or sauce, from either your fridge or your pantry.

Find a spread to enhance whatever main ingredients you're about to layer over the top. Will savory or sweet underline things well?

Place your spread on the toast.

Add the main ingredients—one, or a couple that make good partners.

Choose a topping that will set everything off.

Broil open-faced if that will finish things well. Or warm in a microwave or oven. Or serve at room temperature or chilled.

MAKING TOAST TOPPERS AND MORE

- **Look for ways of making bits and pieces** from the fridge into melts. Simply layer some vegetables onto toast, maybe spoon a little sauce over (white sauce is a super helper with leftovers), then add a layer of cheese. Stick it in the toaster oven or under the broiler until it's good and hot and melty. It's really great with a few rings of onion on top of the cheese; they turn brown and fragrant in the heat. —MARGARET

- **The right kind of leftovers** can definitely spruce up a sandwich. In summer, you might roast a lot of eggplant for eggplant Parmesan or to enjoy it as a side dish. Roasted eggplant slices enhance just about any kind of sandwich filling. (Aim to make an extra slice or two of eggplant whenever you're roasting.) You could add sauerkraut to just about any sandwich, too. It's delicious. —DARYL

Lorre shared these great ideas:

- **Almost anything can fill a tortilla wrap.** Put chopped leftover meat in a wrap, then top it with fresh lettuce, plain Greek yogurt or sour cream, and grated cheese. Or spread all of that over half of a flat tortilla with whatever else you like (cooked onions, asparagus, green beans, etc.). Fold it over and butter or oil both sides. Toast it in a hot skillet like you would a grilled cheese sandwich or pop it into a toaster oven.

- **Heat hard taco shells** in a toaster oven. Fill them with meat or veggies that you have on hand.

Impromptu Tartines

There are so many things to do with toasts—or *tartines*, as the French call them. But we're simply talking about a piece of toast with several savories piled on top, which you can run under the broiler if you want.

I often start with any green vegetable I have on hand and sauté it with a bit of onion or garlic. I lay it down on a platform of an interesting jam or sauce I find in the fridge, then top it with a layer of cheese.

I keep tomato jam on hand partly for this purpose, and one year I made onion jam from an overabundance of onions. Sautéed mushrooms are great as a base or main ingredient, as is sauerkraut mixed with a bit of grated Swiss cheese and a home-made Thousand Island dressing that I stir up myself using ketchup, mayo, and pickle relish.

Or I put baked beans on toast in the English way. I sometimes add a soft-fried egg to any of the above for protein. Or I make classic grilled cheese but then pull the sandwiches open when they're done frying and stuff vegetables or slaw into them just before serving.

What follows are ideas to kick off your imagination.
Interchange and swap and think of completely new ways to top
toast or a flatbread or fill a sandwich, wrap, tortilla, or taco. Use
leftovers whenever you have them on hand.

SALAD ON TOAST

1. **Mix mayo** with a dash of balsamic vinaigrette.
2. **Spread the balsamic mayo** on bread or toast.
3. **Pile on a leafy salad** made of greens with personality, tomato cubes, peach chunks, and broken pieces of fresh mozzarella.
4. **Top with slivered almonds** (toasted, if you have the time).

FRUIT AND MEAT HARMONY

1. **Spread apricot jam** on flatbread.
2. **Add slices** (no more than ¼ inch thick) of leftover cooked ham, unpeeled fresh apple slices, and Brie. Fold the flatbread over.
3. **Place the flatbread** in a skillet or panini press and brown on both sides until the cheese melts.

DO YOU HAVE A TUNA OR CHICKEN SALAD you like a lot? Substitute your favorite cooked beans for the meat, and you've got a new delicious filling.
—DARYL

Berries for
Breakfast

BERRIES FOR BREAKFAST

1. **Toast sourdough bread slices** until just crispy.

2. **Mix ricotta** and honey. Spread over the toast.

3. **Lay sliced strawberries** or whole blueberries or raspberries on top, or a combo of berries.

BREAKFAST TOAST

1. **Toast** multigrain bread.

2. **Spread Greek yogurt** or a creamy cheese on top of the toast.

3. **If you're using cheese,** broil the toast until the cheese bubbles.

4. **Spoon a layer** of toasted broken pecans, hazelnuts, or your favorite mixture of nuts over the top.

5. **Drizzle** with honey.

LEFTOVERS REARRANGED

1. **Toast** your favorite bread.

2. **Cover the toast** with orange marmalade.

3. **Top** with leftover roasted broccoli, bits of cooked ham, brown mustard, and melty cheese.

4. **Broil** until the cheese bubbles and browns.

GREEN, WHITE, AND RED PARTNERS

1. **Spread miso** or hummus on your favorite bread (toasted or not).

2. **Thinly slice unpeeled zucchini** (raw or cooked) lengthwise and make a bed of it on the bread. Stud it with thin slices of radishes. Salt and pepper freely.

3. **Pile on watercress** or fresh baby spinach.

4. **Top with a slice** of well-buttered bread (toasted or not).

toast toppers and their cousins

DEFINITELY-NOT-BLAND BEANS

1. **Toast sturdy bread** until crisp.

2. **Mix cooked and drained beans** with tomato paste or a thick tomato sauce, finely chopped onions and/or garlic, salt and freshly ground black pepper to taste, and any herbs that you like to amp up the flavor a bit. Spoon over the toast.

3. **Top with grated mozzarella** or Swiss cheese.

4. **Broil** until the cheese bubbles and browns.

Easy and Delicious Bean Paste

I learned to eat refried bean sandwiches in Latin America. Beans are easy to make and easy to mash into a spreadable paste.

If you have an electric pressure cooker or a multicooker, beans go quickly from hard and dry to edible and come out much better than canned beans from the store. Add some garlic, a little ground cumin, and salt to the dried beans. Set them to pressure-cook for 25 to 30 minutes, and voilà.

While the beans cook, sauté some onions and a garlic clove or two. Add them to the softened beans and mash everything together with a fork or potato masher or in a food processor.

Use the delicious result as filling for enchiladas or spread it on toast. Or stir a little sour cream into the filling, spoon it over bread, and top it with fresh lettuce and/or cilantro, plus a slice of onion, to make a delicious sandwich. —DARYL

FOUR VEGETABLES AND A MEAT

1. **Toast** your favorite bread.

2. **Smash an avocado** and spread it on the toast. Salt lightly.

3. **Top** with red onion slices, leftover cooked turkey slices (no more than ¼ inch thick), tomato slices, and lettuce.

4. **Drizzle** with honey-mustard dressing.

toast toppers and their cousins

WINTERTIME CAPRESE

1. **Toast slices** of good sourdough or a baguette.

2. **Spread a thick layer** of pesto on the toasted bread.

3. **Top** with sun-dried tomatoes and fresh spinach leaves.

4. **Add sliced fresh mozzarella** or grated mozzarella.

5. **If you're using grated mozzarella,** broil the toast until the cheese melts and bubbles. If you're using fresh mozzarella, consider making it a sandwich, spreading the top piece of toast with Dijon mustard or more pesto.

EGGS AND TOAST HAVE COMPANY

MAKE SCRAMBLED EGGS AND TOAST for suppertime guests, especially unexpected ones. It's easy to make as much as you need of this crowd-pleaser, and you've got a whole meal if you have a veg and/or fresh or canned fruit on hand to go with it.

—MARGARET

1. **Make egg salad** with chunked hard-cooked eggs, chopped celery, minced onion, dill or other fresh herbs, mayo, salt, and freshly ground black pepper. Taste. Add a little mustard if something's missing, or maybe a bit more salt.

2. **Toast two pieces** of your favorite bread.

3. **Spoon the egg salad** over one piece of toast.

4. **Top with sliced fresh tomatoes** and a thin layer of lettuce.

5. **Spread mayo** on the second piece of toast, then place on top.

Wintertime
Caprese

Good &
Pretty

GOOD & PRETTY

I LOVE A BACON AND MARMALADE SANDWICH on toasted pumpernickel for a balance of salty and sweet, and a great texture feast!
—GINI

1. **Toast** your favorite bread.

2. **Spread berry jam** on the toast.

3. **Top** with cooked leftover turkey (not too thick), fresh apple slices, and cooked asparagus.

4. **Grate a hard-cooked egg** over the asparagus.

5. **Squeeze a lemon** over everything.

6. **Decide** whether to add a top slice of bread or to eat it open-faced.

CHEW SLOWLY AND SAVOR

1. **Sauté** some mushrooms. Caramelize some onions, too, if you wish.

2. **Mix horseradish** with mustard.

3. **Spread the horseradish mixture** on toast or a flatbread.

4. **Top** with thin slices of cooked beef. Cover with the sautéed mushrooms and their juice.

5. **Finish** with caramelized onions draped over all, if using, and maybe some pickle slices.

WIDE-AWAKE CHICKEN

1. **Mix mayo** with a drizzle of honey, a few shakes of curry powder, and halved grapes.

2. **Stir small chunks** of cooked chicken and chopped raw celery into the dressing. Taste. Add salt and freshly ground black pepper, if needed, or more honey or curry powder.

3. **Pile the mixture** onto toast or flatbread. Or if you want a sandwich, add a few lettuce leaves and a top slice of bread spread lightly with mayo.

PORK WITH CRUNCH

1. **Split** a sturdy roll. Toast the insides.

2. **Pile the bottom half** of the roll with grilled or roasted shredded pork and a bit of its sauce.

3. **Spoon red or white cabbage slaw** on top. Finish with the top half of the roll.

EGG TACOS

1. **Warm or toast** tortillas.

2. **Scramble some eggs** in butter, along with diced onions and jalapeño.

3. **Stir in shredded cheese** with some sting and cook until softly melted.

4. **Spoon the mixture** into the prepared tortillas.

5. **Top with salsa** and sliced scallions. Squeeze lime juice over all.

FISH TACOS

1. **Season your favorite whitefish** with the flavors you like best. Sauté, bake, or broil just until flaky.

2. **Warm or toast** tortillas.

3. **Break the cooked fish** into pieces with a fork and place it into the prepared tortillas.

4. **Top** with your favorite chopped, crunchy vegetables or slaw.

5. **Spoon sauce** (maybe sour cream and/or mayo, Sriracha, lime juice, and garlic powder) over all.

BEEF TACOS

1. **Warm or toast** tortillas.

2. **Stir ground beef,** onion slices, your favorite taco seasonings, and ketchup or tomato paste together in a hot skillet until browned. Taste. Add whatever flavor you want more of.

3. **Spoon the beef mixture** into the prepared tortillas.

4. **Top** with shredded cheese. Let everything melt together before you take your first bite.

A SAUCE BRINGS IT ALL TOGETHER

1. **Chop leftover cooked vegetables** (carrots, green beans, and others) into small pieces. Add corn and/or peas, too, along with leftover cooked chicken.

2. **Mix the vegetables and chicken** into a white sauce (see page 124) or chicken gravy. Season to taste.

3. **Ladle the mixture** over toast cubes or split biscuits.

toast toppers and their cousins

It's in our

DNA to approach food as a social glue. Humans love to eat together. We can carry this over to food preparation, too. When friends drop by, turn it into a celebration. Invite them to stay for dinner. Welcome them into your busy world. Continue the air of celebration with everyone helping to make the meal— freestyle, of course—that you will eat together! —GINI

Beef Tacos

MELTY CHEESE, FRESH FRUIT, AND CHOCOLATE

1. **Melt thick slices** of mild and creamy cheese over your favorite bread.

2. **Slice pears** (no reason to peel them) and settle them into the squishy cheese.

3. **Drizzle** with melted dark chocolate.

PEANUT AND APPLE BUTTERS WITH FRUIT

I FOUND PEANUT BUTTER WITH HOT PEPPERS in stores in Haiti. I haven't found that for sale in North America, so occasionally I add red pepper flakes to my peanut butter, which sparks up a peanut butter sandwich quite nicely.

—DARYL

1. **Spread peanut butter** over the bottom slice of your favorite sandwich bread.

2. **Spread apple butter** over the top slice.

3. **Drop raisins** and halved grapes over the peanut butter.

4. **Top** with unpeeled apple slices and mild cheese slices.

5. **Cover** with the top slice of bread.

INDEX

Page numbers in *italic* indicate photos; numbers in **bold** indicate charts.

C

P

MORE WAYS TO EXPAND YOUR COOKING SKILLS

with Books from Storey

by Kati Neville & Lindsay Ahrens

With these 150 make-ahead dishes, you can cook one bulk recipe and have three meals for four ready in your freezer. You'll never worry about dinner again!

by Elisabeth Bailey

Transform your weeknight dinners with these 62 make-ahead, freezer-friendly sauces. Flavor-packed classics like All-American Barbecue and Sausage Ragu join creative options such as Chorizo Garlic, Pumpkin Coconut Cream, and Gorgonzola-Chive Butter.

by Stacie Billis

Discover 50 winning recipes for easy, flavorful chicken dishes prepared on the stove or grill, in the oven, or in an Instant Pot.

Join the conversation. Share your experience with this book, learn more about Storey Publishing's authors, and read original essays and book excerpts at storey.com. Look for our books wherever quality books are sold or call 800-441-5700.